AF574143

The performing world of the actor

actor

The performing world of the

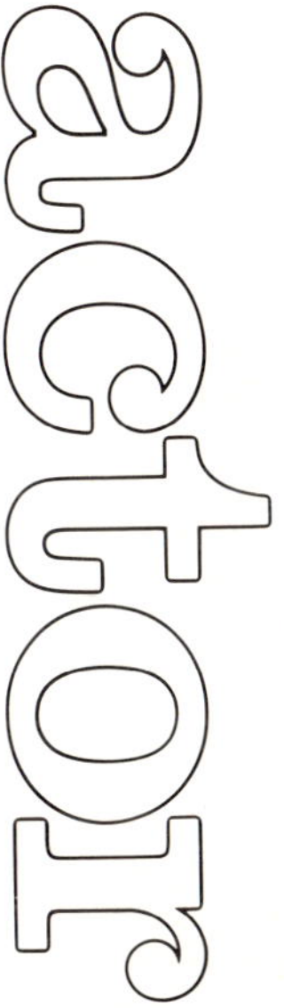

Clive Swift

with a profile of
Glenda Jackson

Hamish Hamilton
London

For my sister Eve, who made me love Theatre

Designed and produced by Breslich & Foss, London

Design: Leslie & Lorraine Gerry
Picture Research: Mary Corcoran
House Editors: Deborah Mainwaring/Timothy Seward
Interviews: Pamela Harvey

First published in 1981
by Hamish Hamilton Children's Books
Garden House, 57–59 Long Acre, London WC2E 9JZ

British Library Cataloguing in Publication Data

Swift, Clive
The performing world of the actor.
1. Acting—Juvenile literature
I. Title
792'.028 PN2065

ISBN 0-241-10585-4

Filmset and printed in Great Britain by
BAS Printers Limited, Over Wallop, Hampshire
and bound by Leighton Straker

Contents

On the Stage

1

Singing and dancing are probably as old as hunting and giving birth. Primitive people still hold ceremonies of celebration after a successful hunt or perform dances asking their gods to ease the rain or hide the sun. Drama—which just means 'happenings'—is one of mankind's ways of showing high emotion. When birth or death or important events occur some kind of ceremony can release our feelings. Agrarian societies, which depended upon weather and crops for survival, naturally came to develop religions and invent deities to protect the well-being of the tribe. These people thought singing and dancing and dressing up as a representation of a god or goddess might influence the abundance of the harvest or the harshness of the winter. Drama, plays, emerged out of these key moments in the lives of human beings.

The First Plays and Actors

The first written plays that we possess are Greek. In Athens, nearly five hundred years before the birth of Christ, play competitions were held in honour of Dionysus, the god of Fertility. They were performed on a flat piece of ground with the audience looking down from a hillside, and the best plays were awarded prizes. The plays often obeyed certain rules, known as the 'unities', which meant that a single story had to happen at one time and in one place. There were

Next to the sacred Temple of Apollo (the pillars on the left) and under the shadow of Mount Olympus the Greeks built this amphitheatre at Delphi. This is how it stands today. What finer setting for great drama!

two forms of play: tragedy, which dealt with serious subjects and important people, and comedy, which lampooned the great and was often very rude. Aeschylus, Sophocles and Euripides were the most famous writers of tragedy, and Aristophanes of comedy. These Greek dramatists developed the forms used by all subsequent European playwrights. Ancient Romans, Spanish, English, German, Americans and Scandinavians have tried to write as well since.

In ancient Greece wayside stages existed. These 'booth' theatres were portable; players carried their theatre round the streets and someone collected money from the crowd even as the show went on. Although acting for a living was an uncertain way of life, many Greek actors were lucky because the ones chosen to play in tragedy and comedy in the large arenas were paid by the state or by rich patrons. In order to earn their keep they had to train at posture, voice production, female impersonation, singing and dancing.

The Greek classical actor performed in the open air to about fifteen thousand people. The central characters in a play were few and the main part was taken by the large chorus, sometimes amounting to fifty men. All Greek actors were men; women were barred from taking acting parts. Every actor wore a mask, no

There is plenty of room for the actor's voice to come out of this Greek comic mask

matter what character he was playing, and some specialized in playing women's roles.

Thespis of Icaria was a playwright as well as an actor and he realized that by wearing different masks the same actor could play more than one part. (Thespis has given his name to the acting profession: you will still hear actors called 'thespians'.) And so, gradually, more and more individual characters came to appear in plays, while the chorus, which had begun its life as by far the most important element, came finally to provide merely light relief between the five tragic acts. By the time Euripides was writing, Greek drama was primarily about individuals, although kings and queens were still the main characters.

The tragic actor wore a bold mask with a crude, fixed expression of the character he was playing, made of light wood or cork and canvas. He also wore high-soled boots and padding underneath his brightly coloured robes. Thus the large audience could see the leading players and know who was speaking at any time. The chief protagonists kept still while the chorus sang and danced around them. In serious drama the Greek chorus mirrored the action of the play by their concern or happiness at what was going on. Athens was a democracy and through the chorus the best playwrights reflected the people's concern about what their rulers were doing and whether they were making the right decisions or not. Often the theatrical arena served a similar purpose to our radio or television when it broadcasts political debate: the nation could hear and judge its leaders. In fifth century Athens, constantly at war with the Persians, the whole town could be informed about what was going on through the awareness and wisdom of its playwrights.

Comedy was an excuse to have a carnival in hard times. The comic masks reflected this licence and crudity. Clowns belched and fell on their behinds and wore a 'prop' phallus. However, Aristophanes' social satires were brilliantly witty as well.

Athens produced great men and great ideas but this 'golden age' did not last long and by about 200 B.C. the all-conquering Romans had begun to set their predatory hands on the glory that was Greece.

The Roman Theatre

Rome had a large empire and built many splendid amphitheatres within her territories. If you go to Orange in southern France or Merida in Spain you will see them still standing. The Romans built long platform stages and sat their audiences on tiered stone. They also built permanent stone scenery running along the back of the stage which helped to focus the audience's eye on the actors and provided the players with exits, entrances and an upper level that could be used as a balcony or a place from which to ambush a victim.

Though at least one actor, Roscius, grew rich and famous, most performers' lives were hard and

A Greek actor of Tragedy would have worn this costume. Note the platform shoes, the anguished mask and the whole pose of fear

managers were forced to stage popular entertainments in order to earn a living. The Romans had little taste for serious plays; they preferred gladiator fights, chariot races or the water ballets when the theatres were flooded and girls in 'bikinis' swam. Most actors came from the slave-class; women, however, were still not allowed to act in plays. Masks were used and female impersonation was the custom.

A model reconstruction of the Roman theatre at Orange in southern France. The permanent scenery is very elaborate and the actors have some protection from the rain

Plautus and then Terence were the most popular writers of comedies, and through them and the southern Italian *fabula atellana* (a peasant drama), the characters and situations that form the content of most comedy were shaped. Two young lovers, an angry father, a shrewish wife and a muddled slave came to be the 'stock-types' that provided the nucleus of plays and determined the formation of an acting troupe. Every ensemble had to have its ingénues, its 'heavies' and its clowns. About a dozen players were needed to tackle material and to tour the countryside, and this number has remained constant from A.D. 200 to the present day. Shakespeare's company and today's average repertory company consist of the same numbers. Fifteen people can play a rounded repertoire of entertainment as well as 'mount' and 'strike' (set up and take down) their productions.

When Seneca, the last classical tragic writer,

wrote his gory tales, he didn't expect them to be performed, so low had sunk the reputation of the Roman theatre and so little was it attended by the intelligentsia. Thus began that habit of reading plays instead of watching them, which often makes for an incomplete understanding of the nature of theatre. But Rome's days were numbered as Christianity arose and barbarian tribes destroyed the capital. The poor actors fled from the invaders and from the disapproval of the Christian Church. They wandered Europe getting employment where they could, at the houses of the rich who still enjoyed after-supper amusement. Printing had not yet been invented and it is important to realize that a nation's culture was still carried by the singers of songs and the tellers of tales. Mimes, musicians and jesters did more than entertain people throughout thc so-called Dark Ages: together with the Church, which hoarded the Latin and Greek texts of books and plays, they preserved culture.

The Mystery and Miracle Plays

The Christian Church condemned all drama as being profane and licentious. Certainly Roman drama had become pornographic, and the Christian duty lay in promoting the work and life of Jesus. The priests little realized that they held the world's most famous drama in their liturgy. But a world without theatre seeks it anywhere, and Christ's resurrection, even in its church-service form, showed the first chink of light in a dramatically starved time. Priest and choirboys would enact the arrival of the women at Christ's tomb, and it wasn't long before other moments in the Christian Passion were given dramatic life. Soon the story of the Nativity and the Crucifixion was moved outside the churches; the staging had grown too elaborate and the content too vulgar for a place of worship. The new drama flourished in the streets and produced a vast repertoire. Plays were written on all biblical subjects, from both the Old and New Testaments, and ordinary people seized upon this opportunity to be creative and to do God's work at the same time. They wrote the plays, built the scenery, played the roles and vied with one another to mount the best productions.

These 'Mystery' plays, as they were called, flourished throughout Europe, each nation making its own common language version from the Latin bible. In fact, local writers embellished the stories richly: amusing characterization was given to Noah's wife, or to the shepherds watching their flocks by night. In England several large towns produced their own collections (cycles) of these Mystery plays. They initiated a new way of presenting drama. Each story in the Bible had a separate wagon, scenery and group of actors to itself. Having performed in one place, the company would go down the street and perform in another. A spectator could stand in one place and watch the whole sequence of Bible stories pass before him in a day.

A religious play at Coventry—perhaps part of the Coventry Mystery 'cycle'—performed in a pageant cart on wheels. The men with the rope help move it from place to place. The emblem embroidered on the drape suggests the production has been staged by the Guild of Carpenters (a kind of early trade union)

The Mystery plays still provide an ever-fresh telling of the Bible stories. Listen to this, from the Wakefield Cycle. The three simple shepherds have come to the newborn Jesus with their gifts:

1st: HAIL, COMELY AND CLEAN! HAIL YOUNG CHILD
HAIL, MAKER, AS I MEAN, OF MAIDEN SO MILD!
LO! HE LAUGHS, MY SWEETING,
A WELCOME MEETING:
TAKE MY PROMISED GREETING,
HAVE A BOB OF CHERRIES.

2nd: HAIL, I KNEEL AND COWER! A BIRD I HAVE
BROUGHT
BAIRN THAT YE ARE.
HAIL LITTLE TINY MOP
OF OUR CREED THOU ART TOP.

3rd: HAIL DARLING DEAR, FULL OF GODHEAD!
HAIL, HOLD FORTH THY HAND SMALL:
I BRING THEE BUT A BALL.
HAVE THOU AND PLAY WITHALL
AND GO TO THE TENNIS.

Where else is the infant Jesus addressed so naturally and fondly? And where else would he be encouraged to become a tennis player!

Amateur actors, not professionals, were involved in staging these plays and the 'Miracle' plays too, written about non-biblical subjects but also dealing with religious experiences. Never again have 'ordinary' people helped to spread so much theatre. In Europe, these plays occupied the minds and labours of people for centuries.

Professional directors may have been brought in to organize some of these elaborate shows, with their hand-woven garments, their carefully made scenery and complicated mechanics, as when Jonah lived in the whale's belly or guilty souls were tossed into the 'Hell Mouth' on Judgement Day. Comedy intertwined with seriousness in these religious pieces. 'Interludes' became popular: short everyday plays done to contrast with the overall solemnity of God's design. The 'Morality' play, where Good and Evil fought and the Seven Deadly Sins came to life, also prospered in times which were harsh and disease and sickness rife. Christian morality offered some explanation for man's suffering. Gradually the professional player could earn a living again, taking

The big cast of a French Miracle Play—'The Martyrdom of Saint Apolline'. The director holds a book and a baton to give instructions to his angels, musicians, torturers and devils who hope that the Saint's soul is coming their way

plays to court and to the rich houses. Amateurs after all, cannot leave hearth and home for long.

The Renaissance

In the great cities of Italy a new spirit arose, inspired by the ancient classical tradition. Men thought that Greece and Rome had created all that was best in the arts, and powerful princes encouraged the building of palaces, execution of paintings and composition of music. The Renaissance flowered here and spread throughout Europe. Drama soon reached great heights—but it grew from popular roots. The *Commedia dell'arte*, a mixture of old Roman comedy and the *fabula atellana*, captured the imagination of

Talented and lively players of a *Commedia dell'arte* troupe showing their varied skills. The masks they wore were often made from leather

Italians and was shortly to be seen in France, Spain, England and Germany.

The *Commedia dell'arte* may be translated as 'professional theatre' and perhaps never before or since has so much depended upon the skills of individual performers. Troupes would set up their booth stages in the squares of Florence, Venice or Naples and entertain all classes of people by their songs, acrobatics and wit. Stock characters like Arlecchino and Colombina (later Harlequin and Columbine of pantomime), Pantalone (the old man), Braggadoccio (the boasting soldier) and various comic servants (called Zanni) appeared in every play, and from such standard characters many variations of plot and situation were devised. We have hundreds of *Commedia* playscripts but none has much dialogue. The *Commedia* players were masters of improvisation and made up the words as they went along! But they always had favourite tricks or pieces of 'business' which they worked into the story, and some of these traditional routines can still be seen at the circus or pantomime. Every actor could sing, dance and play an instrument besides being able to improvise dialogue and tumble expertly. The Gelosi were a leading troupe (whose leading lady, Isabella Andreini, was seen in England), and no matter what countries they visited, the *Commedia* always proved an inspiration to the native theatre-folk. Their usual make-up was a mask (the mask is such an efficient and complete transformation), and indeed the stock characters were known as Masks. You might assume the mask of Scaramouche or Il Dottore all your life. The best talents became known as the characters they played. The *Commedia dell'arte* influenced Shakespeare's *Comedy of Errors* and *The Taming of the Shrew*, indeed they influenced all western theatre. Even Mr. Punch of *Punch and Judy* originated as Pulcinella, the foolish hunchback of the *Commedia.*

The Elizabethan Age

While opera began to hold the interest of the Italian aristocracy and ornate theatres sprang up in Milan and Ferrara, Spain and England were developing a more democratic drama, played in inn-yards or in the *corrales* (courtyards) between blocks of houses. In 1576 James Burbage erected Britain's first purpose-built theatre, called The Theatre, and he had to build it outside the precincts of the city of London because no licence was given him. The Theatre was tower-shaped and unroofed. It did well and soon other theatres appeared in the capital. Now was the time when the living stage showed all that it could do, for Spain and England were thriving empires and their playwrights able enough to reflect expanding and inquisitive societies. America had recently been discovered and the earth's globe was known to be round. Shakespeare's company owned The Globe Theatre at Bankside in Southwark, and with its open roof, its timber stage and its dark vaults it resembled a true microcosm of planet earth (spinning, as Galileo was soon to swear, around the fiery sun).

The Elizabethans enjoyed life and were proud; proud to defeat Spain's Catholic Armada, and arrogantly unaware that in Madrid a theatre was flourishing nearly equal to that of Marlowe, Shakespeare and Ben Jonson. Lope de Vega wrote 750 plays

The only contemporary illustration of an Elizabethan theatre—The Swan, which stood near Shakespeare's Globe at Bankside. The seating (*Sedilia*) would have carried on all the way round; and notice the 'Actors only' area (*mimorum œdes*). The flag and trumpeter advertise the show to the passing public

and Calderon perhaps 200. Shakespeare managed only 37, but everyone would agree that more than half of them are universal masterpieces.

It was the public's demand that made writers so prolific, and for actors (of whom Shakespeare was one) this was a hectic time. Players banded together to put their money into theatre buildings and finance productions. Mornings were spent rehearsing, afternoons playing and evenings, even if at the tavern, planning or writing. When the Black Death, the deadly plague, hit London the players would tour the countryside, and often they were invited to court where the Master of the Revels had the job of providing eminent guests with sumptuous entertainment (although penny-pinching Queen Elizabeth would always make do with less).

In Shakespeare's *A Midsummer Night's Dream* the fairies do everything Donkey-Bottom asks of them, even scratching his face when it itches. Lila de Nobili designed this production for the Royal Shakespeare Company in 1960

William Shakespeare, of course, wrote in verse (which is probably easier to memorize than prose) and it was the superb language of his plays that most appealed to his audience. The Globe Theatre would be thronged with the nobility on stage seats, 'groundlings' pressed up against the three sides of the thrusting platform stage and citizens packed into the galleries. It is reckoned that 2000 people could be squashed into the Globe, though the smell and heat of the sweating bodies would not pass the hygiene laws of today's Health Inspectors! The staging was simple and there was no attempt at historical accuracy in costuming. Actors would make do with 'four or five most vile and ragged foils' (swords) in their battles, and Shakespeare, besides continually apologizing to the audience for the limitations of the theatre (perhaps if he lived now he would make films), beseeched the audience to use their imaginations and let his poetry colour the dawn or the trees or the foaming river he might be talking about.

Shakespeare's plays were rarely published during his lifetime, and then only in single editions for fear that rival companies would pirate the text. The scripts were kept under lock and key and not until 1623 did two actors, working chiefly from prompt-copies and their own memories, give the world the First Folio, an edited collection of thirty-six of Shakespeare's plays which has occupied the minds of actors and scholars ever since.

Neither Shakespeare nor Spain's Lope de Vega paid much attention to the ancient 'rules' of Greek drama. The divisions into five acts and the unities of time, place and action were often swept aside in these new plays. Both dramatists agreed that the audience is always the final judge of success and that the theatre is a practical craft, where only what pleases can stay and what doesn't please must be rejected.

As in Athens, the Elizabethan theatre became a centre of social life. Without newspapers, plays told you what was 'in the air' and anybody might be seen at a playhouse, from foreign ambassador to Catholic spy. Though Ben Jonson's comedies of morals and Shakespeare's great tragedies were written during a mere twenty golden years, Fletcher's lighter plays and Webster's malevolent melodramas continued to draw the townsfolk until Oliver Cromwell's puritans closed all theatres in 1642. Spain's theatre had dwindled and England's was snuffed out.

French Plays and Playwrights

England's actors went abroad and sought gainful employment in Germany or Holland: the English actor's reputation was high. But it was France that produced the next great theatre through the work of Jean Baptiste Poquelin (Molière) and Jean Racine, two very different kinds of playwright. Louis XIV is said to have founded the art of ballet by his patronage and participation, and it was at his court, too, that both Racine's and Molière's plays first saw the light of day. Molière was a complete man of the theatre who had learned his trade in the provinces and now led his own company in his own plays. *Le Misanthrope*, *L'Avare* and *Tartuffe* are three comedies which make serious moral points about how we should live. *Le Bourgeois Gentilhomme* remains the perfect play about the foolishness of social pretension.

Nicola, Monsieur Jourdain's maid, doesn't fight according to the rules but she wins all the same! A scene from Molière's *Le Bourgeois Gentilhomme* in which Madame Jourdain looks very amused at her husband's antics

Unhappily, Molière's plays do not translate well (nor do Racine's), but if your French is good they are there to be performed and enjoyed. Recent French productions have emphasized Molière's realism as well as his humour. Certainly, though he was inspired as writer and performer by the Parisian *Commedia dell'arte* troupe, his work has become as classic, as permanently worthwhile, as that of Shakespeare or Aristophanes.

Jean Racine wrote poetic tragedies and provided actresses with wonderful roles. Like Euripides before him he examined female psychology in great depth, in particular the agony between a queen's public face and her private feelings. Two hundred years before human psychology was studied seriously, Racine, a severely religious man who retired from playwriting in his prime, seemed to understand the motivations of women.

England—New Theatres and Great Actors

King Charles II of England (and Scotland) had been at Louis XIV's court during his French exile and when he returned to London he encouraged the kind of theatre he had seen in France. For the first time,

The Drury Lane theatre was burnt to the ground in 1672 and 1809. It was also bombed during World War II, but each time it has been re-built and still stands today. This is a view from the stage in 1792 showing the 'pit', boxes and galleries which could hold two thousand people

actresses were seen on the London stage and two theatres were specially licensed to perform plays. One of these was the Theatre Royal, Drury Lane, which today is the 'home' of the British musical theatre, and is still under royal patent with a special box and set of rooms for the Royal Family should they wish to attend a performance. The eighteenth century saw theatre become what we know it as now: a variety of playhouses of varying elegance, presenting a various fare. In 1700 London and Paris had merely a handful of theatres, but by 1800 the whole of Europe boasted theatres and large audiences. Drama flourished under the patronage of a growing middle class. City and provincial life encouraged theatre-going as a fashionable pursuit, and theatre managers had to get down to the tricky business of providing entertainment for the whole family.

Theatre buildings changed. They were now roofed, with pretty pillared auditoriums and proscenium arches which divided the stage area from the audience. The 'thrust' stage—the platform jutting well into the audience—was reduced to a shorter

A vivid impression of Garrick as Shakespeare's King Richard III just before he meets his death

'fore-apron' in order to seat more customers. In mid-century orchestra pits appeared. Backstage dressing rooms and a 'green room' were provided where the artists could greet their public. Theatre was now for the fashionable. Quite soon there was a social split between the elegant theatre of the rich and the strolling entertainers who travelled from town to town crying their offerings on the common or (if they could arrange the hire charge) taking over a local theatre for the season—creating rivalry with those installed in the 'legitimate' playhouse! At the top end of the scale was the Theatre Royal, Drury Lane; at the bottom end there were travelling hucksters who could give you performing dogs, a shaky ballet or even 'replicas' of London productions. However, one great actor, the ferocious Edmund Kean, is said to have begun his theatre career with such a troupe run by 'Master John Richardson', the most ambitious and the best of these fit-up managers.

In the mid-eighteenth century, David Garrick, 'a small man of medium height, with flashing expressive eyes' took over the joint managership of Drury Lane. Here he banished the audience from stage seats and introduced concealed lighting and cut-out scenery to

England. Having made his name as Richard III, he shrewdly promoted Shakespeare, and for thirty years Drury Lane stood at the head of world theatre. He was a playwright himself, albeit in an age of poor plays and big 'stars'. ('Peg' Woffington and Kitty Clive—both Irish and both dominating personalities—were two of his leading ladies.) Legally, actors were classed as 'rogues and vagabonds', but Garrick gave them a dignity they had not possessed before. He paid his own company decently, and trained and rehearsed them himself. Molière had been buried in unconsecrated ground but Garrick was buried in Westminster Abbey and mourned by a procession over two miles long.

German theatre, which was only just beginning, played Shakespeare and took Garrick's natural style as a model. Heinrich Heine, Lessing, Goethe and Schiller worked hard to fashion a German drama, despite the fact that Germany was still a cluster of separate principalities. The great actor Friedrich Schröder, a devoted Shakespearian, left a fine tradition of ensemble acting both at Hamburg where he managed a theatre, and in Vienna, which boasted some sparkling plays and burlesque in the nineteenth century.

Melodrama and a New Acting Style

By the time of Garrick's death in 1779 the high comedy style, crowned by Sheridan's *The School for Scandal*, was giving way to French melodrama. The actor had to learn this new way to please his taskmaster, the public. Melodrama, which was to be to the Victorians what sentimental cinema is to us, evolved from the musical accompaniment which had come to form an essential part of many plays. Melodrama laid emphasis on spectacular scenic effects such as snowstorms or floods. Theatres were growing bigger and bigger to make more money for managements and the actors had to project their acting in order to fill distant parts of the huge houses and to portray the crude emotions written into the two-dimensional characters. 'Barnstorming' was the name given to this ranting style, and many provincial playhouses rang to the cries of an orphan wailing for his mother or a bully-lord whipping his servants. The

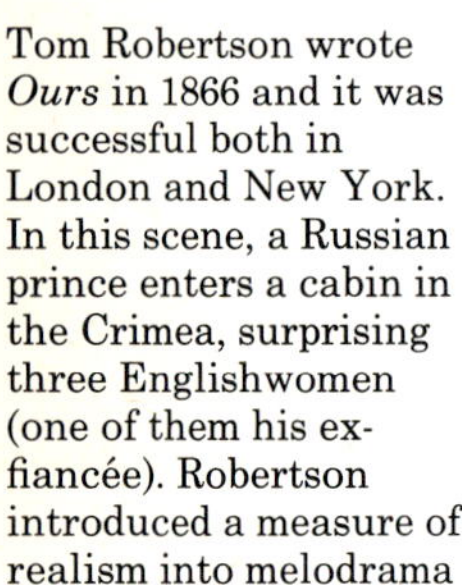

Tom Robertson wrote *Ours* in 1866 and it was successful both in London and New York. In this scene, a Russian prince enters a cabin in the Crimea, surprising three Englishwomen (one of them his ex-fiancée). Robertson introduced a measure of realism into melodrama

cult of horror was strong in the fiction of the early nineteenth century. With its gaslight and its ghostly music the theatre could also chill many a spine up there in 'the gods'.

America, having shaken off her British yoke in 1776, now enters the theatre story. This young, raw country was content at first to imitate its old master and built a theatre in Philadelphia which was copied from Bath's Theatre Royal. Upon its elegant stage the latest London successes were given by ladies and gentlemen clothed in all the fashion of London's Whitehall and Belgravia. New York soon followed suit and built several theatres. The Park, The Chatham and the vast Bowery were among the first.

It wasn't long before a two-way traffic opened up with English and French players crossing the Atlantic to the North and to New Orleans, where a thriving entertainment centre existed. American-born 'stars' bedecked London's nightspots. The first American to act at Drury Lane was the man who wrote the song *Home, Sweet Home*, John Howard Payne. He was quickly followed by the pick of his generation: Junius Brutus Booth, the mountainous Edwin Forrest, Charlotte Cushman and Joseph Jefferson III, who was famous for playing Rip Van Winkle. George Frederick Cooke, Edmund Kean and William Macready, all of them renowned tragedians

To play the Byzantine Empress Theodora, the astonishing Sarah Bernhardt wore a costume sewn with 4,500 gems. This role established her as the French public's top performer

in Britain, went to America; but Cooke's and Kean's excessive drinking and Macready's bitter relationship with Edwin Forrest did little to enhance their reputations. International appearances by 'superstars' were becoming part of the theatre scene. Rachel said farewell at Covent Garden in 1841; Eleonora Duse and Sarah Bernhardt, one Italian and the other French, astonished audiences all over the world with their magnetic artistry. Bernhardt was a silvery-voiced, volatile beauty and Duse an introverted, heavy-lidded romantic. France's Frédérick Lemaître and Italy's Tommaso Salvini were other nineteenth-century players of world stature, as were Britain's Dame Ellen Terry and Sir Henry Irving. These two formed a partnership at London's Lyceum theatre that broke down many stuffy Victorian prejudices against drama. Irving was a curious type

Sir Henry Irving broods as Hamlet, a role that attracts all great actors because it allows great freedom in interpretation

to be an actor, he could just as easily have been an archbishop or a learned judge. He had strange vocal and physical mannerisms, but this distant, clever man attained, with his knighthood, a respect no player had been given before and very few have since. Perhaps only Sir Laurence, now Lord Olivier, has won equal professional and public esteem.

The Music Hall

The fondness for theatre shown by the upper and middle classes was matched by the working man's need and love for the Music Hall. This sort of entertainment started in city taverns, where a man could drink and join in a chorus as he watched, but gradually this 'vaudeville', as the Americans called it, took over theatres. Whole evenings were given over to the commanding personalities that sang, danced and filled the downcast souls of the poor with laughter and joy, so that they were able to face another day at the mill or foundry.

The Victorian Music Hall was witty and wise. It often mocked the high and mighty who ruled not only Britain but a huge empire. Dan Leno, Little Tich,

'Little Tich' (real name Harry Relph) was a star-clown of the Victorian Music Hall. He inspired Charlie Chaplin among others

Sixteen-year-old Bob Hope 'hoofs it' in Vaudeville. He went on to be a film star and a master stand-up comedian

Florrie Forde, Harry Champion, Vesta Tilley and Marie Lloyd are legends in British theatre history, for they were the stars of 'the Halls'. By 1900, in London alone there were over thirty theatres dedicated to Music Hall. It was a variety show, with individuals doing songs or sketches, and a chorus of dancers and singers to 'fill in'. France had cabarets where there was satire and song. The word 'vaudeville' may in fact come from the French 'voix des villes' or songs of the cities. In many countries, artists have triumphed as stand-up comedians or *chanteuses*: Mistinguette and Edith Piaf in France, Bob Hope and Danny Kaye in America, Sir Harry Lauder and George Robey in Britain. They would all know the Music Hall as a unique and wonderful tradition whose spirit should never die. Laughter keeps us sane, and ever since the Middle Ages, the licensed jester has performed a life-giving task.

Theatre flourished in a world that had no other means of professional entertainment. All classes had to be catered for, and it was the Musical which proved most generally popular. Gilbert and Sullivan operettas were the rage in London and were pirated in America. The Viennese waltz kings established a sophisticated and frivolous tradition of musical comedy that was taken up by other countries. England and America sent one another their latest 'hits' (*Floradora* or *The Belle of New York*) and many a chorus girl married into the aristocracy. The beautiful Lily Langtry enjoyed the favour of a King—Edward VII.

New Influences

There were other movements afoot in the theatre at the turn of the nineteenth century. Electric lighting had transformed stage scenery. At the Madison Square theatre the actor and inventor Steele MacKaye amazed his audiences with air-conditioning, an adjustable proscenium and a second stage upon which scenes could be prepared while action took place on the visible one. Technology had entered the business of theatre. Some great playwrights were at work too, and that, finally, determines the importance of the stage in any era.

Russia, which had had theatre from the mid-

Constantin Stanislavsky (arms upraised) acting in the first production of Maxim Gorky's *The Lower Depths* in 1902. Gorky's masterpiece was written from his own raw experience of life

eighteenth century when the Empress Catherine turned playwright, was beginning to understand the division between rich and poor in her society. Anton Chekhov wrote plays about the waning of the middle class, and Maxim Gorky showed the world what it was like to be down and out with no hope. When Karl Marx wrote *Das Kapital* and socialism became a force among intellectuals as well as militants, modern political theatre was born. Beneath his entertaining humour, the sharp-edged wit of England's George Bernard Shaw was advocating a fairer society. If the Moscow Arts Theatre led the way in terms of the craft of acting, France, Germany and England had equally committed men of ideas working in serious theatre. There was a split between audiences who wanted escapism and audiences who wanted to know more about the real world; actors now had to choose in which kind of theatre they wanted to work.

Directors now played an essential part in theatre. In Germany, the Duke of Saxe-Meiningen mounted classical productions where each member of the crowd was characterized and the costumes were historically accurate. Irving had real rabbits in a Lyceum production of *A Midsummer Night's Dream*. This was a trend which started with John Philip Kemble and Charles Kean in London. The old stage-manager methods of control became impractical as too much money was at stake, and actors were hired only for short periods.

Realism versus Expressionism

Constantin Stanislavsky and Nemirovich-Danchenko were joint directors of the Moscow Arts Theatre. Together, they brought a much truer realism to the theatre. Stanislavsky revolutionized the art of acting. He was the first analyst of the craft and insisted that real life was where actors should go to shape their performances. He took his actors to the slums of Moscow before they appeared in Gorky's *The Lower Depths*, and he would rehearse for months in order to give minute naturalistic detail to Chekhov's plays. To some extent his emphasis upon 'reality' was in opposition to the melodramatic style that was still in vogue.

Stanislavsky's methods have infiltrated the

One of the world's greatest playwrights, Anton Chekhov, reads his play *The Seagull* to members of the Moscow Arts Theatre in 1899 including: (next to him on either side) Olga Knipper, an actress who became his wife, and Stanislavsky; and (extreme left) Nemirovich-Danchenko. A seagull is still the emblem of the company

twentieth century, especially the cinema where the close-up camera can record the actor's total relaxation and sincerity, unlike the stage, with its physical distance between performer and audience. America seized upon Stanislavsky's teaching (sometimes misunderstanding it) but the European actor has remained less happy about complete subjectivity in performance. When you act eight times a week you need a cold technique in order not to exhaust yourself or lose your voice. After all, the actor is not only the character but also himself.

Bertolt Brecht, a German playwright and director, insisted that his actors distance themselves from the part they were playing so as to present it to the audience in a critical way: a mask rather than a face. He and Ernst Toller and the Russian Vsevolod Meyerhold, who had started with Stanislavsky's company, began to promote Expressionism during the 1920s. In this kind of theatre the individual character was not important because Man was seen as merely a small cog in an industrial society. Human emotions were symbolically expressed by lighting and scenery. Often individuals were reduced to numbers or ants, as in Karel Čapek's *Insect Play*. This was partly a reaction to Stanislavsky's excessive realism.

The 'depression' of the 1930s and then World War II radically changed people's lives and changed the role of the actor. At home entertainers kept theatre alive in the worst possible circumstances; they also went out to cheer up the soldiers, often in the front line.

Theatre Today

The past thirty years have given actors and actresses the opportunity to perform in cinema, television and radio as well as on the stage. Leading artists of many nations have been able to exercise their talents in all three fields. Orson Welles, Fredric March and Paul Muni have been renowned screen actors as well as theatre giants. Alec Guinness, Laurence Olivier and Michael Redgrave are all film-stars as well as leaders of their profession. Glenda Jackson, Peter O'Toole, Jack Lemmon and Vanessa Redgrave have recently established themselves at the top of both stage and cinema. But this does not happen to all talents.

Screen actors can be ineffective on the stage, and vice versa. Have Jack Nicholson and Robert Redford done many plays? Have Paul Scofield and Judi Dench done many films?

Of late, America and Britain have had vibrant activity in the theatre. Arthur Miller and Tennessee Williams lead the American playwrights and John Osborne and Harold Pinter the British. The Royal Shakespeare Company and the National Theatre are recent additions to the British scene, while Joe Papp's free theatre in Central Park has been a blessing to New York. However, in England, there is little money to subsidize 'art'. Only the 'fringe' theatre, which is able to stage professional productions inexpensively, can afford to experiment. Although London still has a great deal to offer and can rely on tourists to swell the audience, provincial theatre is in a bad way. In America things are more hopeful; musical and 'serious' theatre have merged to form new audiences. Because the nation is so huge each big town is proud to have a playhouse and rightly proud of the new work it produces.

Paul Scofield wears eighteenth-century court dress to play Antonio Salieri in Peter Shaffer's play *Amadeus*. In this play Salieri envies the composer Mozart's genius and is suspected of poisoning him

Cinema

2

Early Days

When the cinema became popular it provided actors and actresses with an important new field of employment; but it took all of fifty years before the all-colour, stereophonic-sound epic reached the screen. The very first moving pictures in 1895 were amusement-parlour peepshows where you put a penny in the slot, cranked a handle and were thrilled to see comedians throwing custard pies at one another, or a heavily corseted lady slipping off her dress. These kinetoscopes were considered a novelty, even by the businessmen and inventors who owned them. They had no idea that cinema would become a potent force in entertainment and education. It could be said that films have equalled books as an influence upon our minds.

It was the poor and young who enjoyed the early 'flickers'; the middle classes wouldn't be seen dead in the sleazy dark rooms with their bench seats and noisy music. But the nickelodeon managers wooed the well-to-do with 'family' programmes and specially filmed scenes from current stage successes. There was no sound; the 'story' was told by 'legends' written in words. Nor was there any attempt to vary the camera angle or even change the distance from which the action was 'shot'. All was as you might see it from a theatre stall. The players merely did what they did on the stage: round eyes, big gestures and all.

A Frenchman, Georges Méliès, experimented with the new miracle of film and discovered such techniques as the 'fade', 'dissolve' and slow and fast motion. His *Cinderella* was the first movie to tell a story with a beginning, middle and end. Yet it was David Wark Griffith, an actor from Kentucky, who created the feature film almost single-handed. This is a film that has a story, and he used the flexibility of the camera to tell the tale. Griffith used the long-shot, mid-shot, and close-up in a pattern of filming which is still used today. In *Intolerance* and *Birth of a Nation* his 'tracking' long shots could reveal whole communities, while his close-ups could expose the human grief or happiness of an individual. He realized that it was the rhythm of the film, the way it was put together in the cutting-room, that was the key to tension and drama. His cameraman, Billy Bitzer, was the first in a line of artists whose work has not been sufficiently praised.

The First Stars

By now film 'stars' had arisen, many of whom had had no stage experience at all. Their faces, their screen personalities held great appeal for the massive audiences which were building up. Winsome girls like Blanche Sweet and Mary Pickford began to command huge salaries at the studios where they were employed. 'All-American' clean young men like

A scene from D. W. Griffith's film *Broken Blossoms* with Donald Crisp and the young Lillian Gish

Douglas Fairbanks, Senior had their photographs pinned up in factories and offices throughout the world. In Hollywood, a rural spot in California where the weather was fine all year round, Mack Sennett set up a troupe of comedians to make hundreds of short comic films. Charlie Chaplin and Stan Laurel began with Sennett. The whole gang were excellent *farceurs*, skilled in the old *commedia* tricks of falls, chases, mime and mimicry. Many were from the Music Hall, and in time Harold Lloyd, Buster Keaton and Oliver Hardy followed in their cinematic footsteps.

Charlie Chaplin was a brilliant mime, a talent which was a great asset in the days of silent cinema. Here he is 'the little man' trying to keep up appearances. Chaplin was not only a clown but a serious actor who made his own films

The Jazz Singer attracted huge crowds at its premiere in 1927

The 'Talkies'

When *The Jazz Singer* was made, with three songs sung by 'black-faced' Al Jolson, and a snatch of dialogue, a change came over the industry which affected it profoundly. 'Sound' was born, and Hollywood celebrated by producing a spate of all-talking, all-dancing-and-singing films which were the first in a line of musicals that other nations could only envy. 'Talkies' now swept the world and some silent stars had to retire to whatever spoils they had amassed. Their voices did not fit their screen image and no matter what money the studios spent on dialogue coaches, German beauties could not lose their foreign accents nor heart-throb males acquire stirring voices. Stage players who were far more skilled in handling words found their way into film. There seemed no bounds to what celluloid could achieve.

The Industry Grows

Cecil B. De Mille typified the new Hollywood. During the economic depression of the 1920s and '30s, he introduced great glamour and luxury into his films. Ordinary people were 'taken out of themselves' by the alluring world they saw on the screen. Ever since, all cinema, but Hollywood in particular, has made it its business to provide the public with dreams. What you can't have or experience in real life the cinema provides for you and, as a result, Hollywood can never lose its tawdry image, its huckster association. It will give you what it thinks you want—at a price. However, many films are made with passion and integrity and Hollywood, too, has produced her fair share of them. Money-making is not the only motive in film-making. Just as, in the theatre, plays are written and staged out of artistic belief, so films are sometimes made in the same way. There seems to be a gap between the commercial film and the art film, although often this divide is bridged. Of course America is not the only country to make films. Most other nations have a proud tradition of cinema, and some of the best movies have come from Italy, France and Britain.

There are many film 'genres' or styles: western, gangster movie, light comedy and war epic, to name but a few. Both world wars encouraged film-making, and during Hitler's war the cinema was able to help the allies' morale by showing great bravery on the screen or reminding people of the peace and happiness they were fighting for. William Holden or Ray Milland inspired the women and Gene Tierney and Barbara Stanwyck the men. They all looked so good

Humphrey Bogart as detective Philip Marlowe in Raymond Chandler's story *The Big Sleep*. With him is actress Martha Vickers

in uniform! And there were many 'super-stars' who seemed to specialize in certain roles: James Cagney and Edward G. Robinson were gangsters, Alan Ladd and John Wayne were cowboys, and Humphrey Bogart was the loner who always seemed to have a cigarette dangling from his lips—so brave, intelligent, tough and tender. What more could you ask?

An International Art

To English-speaking people there is an inevitable drawback in watching foreign films: we can't easily understand the language. However, sub-titles can ease us along and real cinema addicts will know how fine many foreign directors are. Russia, Sweden, France, Italy and Spain have made masterpieces of cinema, and Germany has a brilliant generation of directors at the moment. Film-making is really an international pastime because the producers are after world markets. They might assemble stars from England, Egypt and Peru, a cameraman from Scandinavia and a director from Israel. Then they might shoot the film in Ireland or Africa and do the interior studio scenes in Paris! Huge money is spent on publicity, and money-spinning films are released time and time again for further showing. When their cinema life is finished they are relegated to the television screen. But, for an actor, the pleasant thing about making a film is that it will last a long time. Being filmed is the nearest we can get to immortalizing our work, although even celluloid will eventually crumble.

The Actor's New Role

Film acting is a very different job from acting on the stage. The film caster's philosophy seems to be 'if the face fits . . .'. Only big stars are allowed the indulgence of exploring character on the screen; most actors are cast because they fit the director's notion of the written character. The director often decides whether an actor is right for the part or not as he walks through the door for the first time. It can be very dispiriting.

Unless he has a leading role the actor will not stay long on the film. Every minute costs big money as

there are so many people concerned and so he will be hired to work for only a few days or possibly a few weeks. Rehearsals are for the cameramen, the lighting crew and the director as much as for the actor. He'll be lucky if he gets a film director who is helpful. Many of them were editors or cameramen before they became directors and so they will not have any great experience of actors. But at least an actor can have a second, third or fourth attempt in

Greta Garbo was the cinema's most romantic star. Born in Sweden she spoke English with an accent, photographed beautifully and had an air of wistful yearning. She always kept her private life a secret

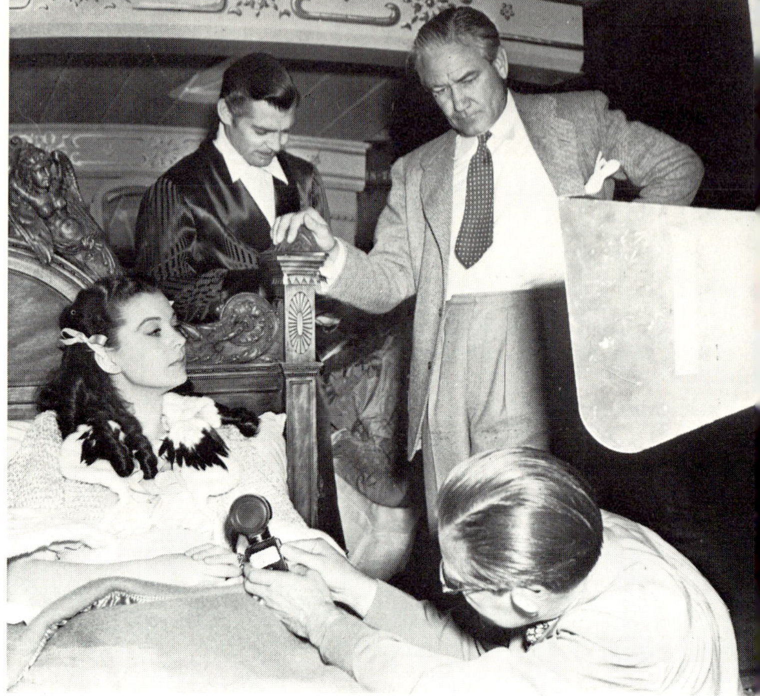

The cameraman takes a light-meter reading before 'shooting' Vivien Leigh in the marathon *Gone With the Wind*. Holding the bedpost is director Victor Fleming and at the back is leading-man Clark Gable. The film grossed $33\frac{1}{2}$ million dollars: one of the all-time biggest money-earners

front of the cameras. Usually these 'takes' are short, and he may be asked to do tiny things like lift one eyebrow an eighth of an inch or purse his lips. That's if he's lucky enough to get a close-up!

He is surrounded by a sea of faces: make-up, wardrobe, assistant-directors, crew. The big lamps are hot. He may stand in the same spot all morning. In the end it is up to the director how much of the actor's role is left in the final version. Unless he is an important star it is not possible for him to have much control over his acting and what the public will finally see. Film-making often seems like a totally scientific process. Laboratories can grade the colour and the tones of the film negative, the sound department can lay an entirely new sound-track on to the film and the editors can cut out whole scenes as long as the story is not muddled. Perhaps it's worth remembering that if a part is concerned with the main plot it is more likely to reach the big screen intact! Yes, it is only in the theatre that the actor has any real measure of control.

Glenda Jackson View from the Top

3

Glenda Jackson is an internationally acclaimed English actress whose success on both stage and screen gives her an exceptional insight into the problems facing young actors and actresses entering the profession in the 1980s. She lives in England but is no stranger to Hollywood, where she has made many successful films.

She established her reputation in the theatre during the early sixties with the Royal Shakespeare Company as well as in such exciting productions as *Marat/Sade*. Her film career has covered a remarkable range of parts from her Oscar-winning role in Ken Russell's *Women In Love* to some lighthearted Hollywood comedies like *A Touch Of Class* with George Segal, for which she won an Academy Award, and *House Calls* with Walter Matthau. She also starred in the highly-praised series *Elizabeth R* on television—a medium in which she doesn't even enjoy working!

Yet despite all her success, Glenda Jackson remains a very down-to-earth person, unimpressed by the trappings of stardom, and a dedicated professional. She brings to the world of 'showbusiness' a sense of realism that is not often evident and that makes her opinions disarmingly honest if at times controversial.

Her attitudes probably stem from the way she herself entered the business. It was hardly the fulfilment of a childhood dream, for Glenda had no interest in drama at all until she was about 17. She never took part in any school productions and can only remember one appearance in a Sunday School Christmas play. 'I played the part of a crippled boy with one line, "A star in the day"!' she laughs.

She left school without any qualifications and was working in Boots the chemists when she and a friend joined a local amateur dramatics group. Her decision to go on from there into the business was taken with astounding naivety—little realizing how difficult it might be.

'Someone said, "You should do this professionally",' she explains, 'and as I was exceedingly dissatisfied with my life at the cash chemists, I wrote to the only drama school I knew of, which was RADA [the Royal Academy of Dramatic Art], and found myself there auditioning.'

Glenda was born and brought up in Cheshire in the north of England so that in fact she was more nervous about going to London than about the audition.

'I had never been away from home before, I was totally ignorant,' she admits, 'although the ignoramus aspect of it was in a way helpful because I just went along, presented myself, did the audition and left immediately.'

However, her talent must have been obvious because she won a place. There was still a problem, for she couldn't afford to pay the fees. So she applied for a scholarship and went back to London for a second audition.

'Then the drama school wrote to my education authority and said that they didn't have a scholarship for that term, but if they had they would have given me one. So my education authority—in those balmy days of largess—paid for all my fees and gave me a very sizeable grant, which kept me in London for the two years I was at drama school.'

For the first term she stayed with relatives and then moved into digs in Kew where she was looked after by her landlady, Mrs Hill, who was like a second mother. Nevertheless, Glenda is aware that her parents were very concerned about her.

'I was the eldest child, the first one to go, and no one had ever lived in London before. But I think it helped that they knew at least I had money because I'd got the grant.

'Then when I left drama school, my parents went through all that terrible anxiety of seeing me try to get work, being out of work more than I was in and going home with holes in my shoes. It was very hard for them.'

Glenda took her work seriously at RADA and was rewarded for her efforts by being cast in a good part in

Glenda Jackson (in *The Romantic Englishwoman*)

an end-of-term production, which led to her being spotted by an agent. Yet she was told not to expect to work much until she was about 40, 'because I was essentially a character actress and there wouldn't be much work for me, which at that time was true.

'I left in 1956 when the British theatre was still mainly commercially oriented. There was male and female lead, male and female juvenile lead, male and female character and male and female juvenile character—and I didn't fit into any of those categories. So it was a fairly accurate assessment of my employment prospects when I left.'

Despite the bleak future predicted for her at that time, Glenda still felt that the time spent at drama school was excellent preparation for an acting career.

'I think the essential thing was that you learned you are your own instrument and that it's up to you to keep that instrument in as good trim as possible—physically and mentally. It's your voice and *you* are all you have to express anything with, and you have to keep it alert, alive and capable of expressing.

'Drama school was also particularly valuable for me,' she adds, 'because I'd never really been with a group of like-minded people before. . . . And, of course, you think you know everything at that stage and the sort of "swingeing" criticism everybody went in for was very stimulating.'

Glenda is extremely modest about herself, for she puts it down to good fortune that she got an agent through that end-of-term show and began working so quickly. However, the change of climate which occurred in the British theatre at that time must have improved her chances of finding suitable roles.

'I think I'd been home about a fortnight and then I got a job with Worthing rep [repertory company] for about two months. I was in *Separate Tables* and *Doctor In The House* and I was deeply distressed because they didn't ask me to stay and become a permanent member of the company.'

After that she went to Hornchurch rep and then to Crewe, where she did everything from ASMing (assistant stage manager) to playing small parts. Nowadays there are very few repertory companies left in Britain, a fact that Glenda sincerely regrets.

'I think it was the best teaching that you can ever have and I think it's terribly sad, in a way, that that particular form of education is not there anymore for young actors. There are still some reps, but there aren't enough of them to provide the right amount of experience for the enormous number of people who want to act.'

She dismisses television experience as a substitute because she says there you only learn how to be a television actor, nothing else. 'Acting on the stage fits you to act in all media, but the other media don't fit you to act on the stage.'

After Crewe, despite her agent and her extraordinary talent, Glenda didn't work at all for two years—a state of affairs that she is all too well aware will dominate most young actors' lives. Although she escaped relatively lightly, she knows the agonies and problems of 'resting'.

'Because I had no qualifications and no training that I could sell, I always had to take the least well-paid jobs which tended to be shop assistant, waitress, odd bouts when I was very lucky of working somebody's switchboard. You became quite good at lying, pretending you'd be there the rest of your life. And I did a series of dreadfully soul-destroying jobs which were awful at the time, but which I'm now quite grateful that I had to do.'

As a result of her experience, Glenda has one major piece of advice to give to would-be actors and actresses:

'Have something that you can earn yourself a living wage with before you even begin to train as an actor. If you have the intelligence to go to university—*go* to university. If you can't do that and if it's only a shorthand/typing course, *do* it so that at least you can earn yourself a reasonable living wage. Because even if you get into a drama school and even if you go through the two years, you're as likely as not to *not* get your Equity ticket [actors' union card]. And if you don't get your Equity ticket, you can't work.

'So you've got to have something to give you a sense of not always being a beggar, which is how you feel at the beginning. All you want to do is work, but it's hard on the individual because nobody looks at

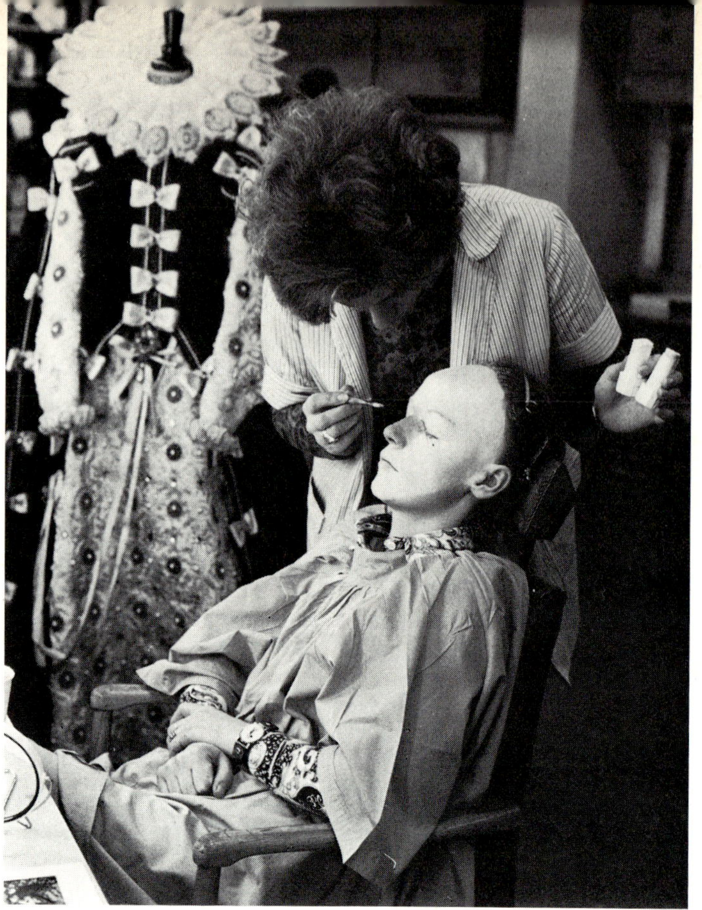

Glenda is made up by Ann Briggs of BBC T.V. to look as she does on the cover of this book: as Queen Elizabeth I of England. Sometimes complicated make-up takes hours and great patience is needed

you like a human being or a person; they're just looking at you as a shape, a colour or as a sound or something—which is very painful.

'It's also difficult to have, riding over you all the time, the possibility that you might not be able to pay the rent or you may need a new pair of shoes and can't afford to buy them. It's important to have something to give you that slight sense of independence which you can only have—and it's obviously going to get worse and worse— if you have some kind of saleable commodity for the job market, and being an actor doesn't give you that.

'I don't think it can be emphasized enough that in a profession as overcrowded as this one is, the chances of you working in any of the allied branches of theatre, film and television are very, very small. So you've got to have something that you can earn a decent, living wage by.'

Glenda also points out that being unemployed is an expensive business for an actor because you have to have certain things in order to stand a chance of getting work. You need a telephone so that you can be reached and photographs of yourself to send out (which are never returned). You need enough money to be able to dress yourself appropriately and you will spend quite a lot on fares getting to auditions which can be all over the place—with no guarantee of success. And all this on top of the basic living expenses!

On the positive side of looking for work, Glenda says that an agent can be extremely helpful—although like all people, there are good, bad and indifferent agents.

'They are immensely useful at the beginning because they do know what is being auditioned—what's being cast—and they do tend to know most of the casting people. The thing is, of course, the casting people have their agents that they know they can trust, so to get a good agent is quite difficult.'

If, unlike Glenda, you are not approached by an agent, you should get a copy of *Contacts* and write to all the agents, enclosing a photo, and follow this up with a personal visit where possible. Then, if you happen to get a job you should write to them again and ask them to come and see you. With luck, in this way you will find one to take you on.

Once you have an agent, as Glenda says, with their contacts you should get more auditions. But she is hardly enthusiastic about this method of finding work.

'I find them horrendous,' she confesses. 'I only ever got one job from doing an audition. Every time they had auditions for the Royal Shakespeare Company, I would be sent along and I would do my little piece and I never got any work from it.

'I think they're crucifying. You can tell absolutely nothing from an audition, which is what is so painful. You go along prepared to act and all they're looking at is your height, your weight, your colour and whether you fit into the scheme of things.'

She also feels that it is even more difficult for girls than it is for men to find work in what she calls the 'serious theatre'.

'The most basic problem is that there are far fewer parts for women and far more actresses, or rather would-be actresses. Women constitute the smallest part of any cast list of any company—think of any television series and there are always fewer women than men. So there's the lack of opportunity of employment.

'Then when you're out of that stage and in the position that you're actually offered work as opposed to pursuing it, you run into the absolute dearth of decent parts to play. They may be long but they're never interesting.'

Having talked about the depressing aspects of life facing a young actor or actress, it is still obvious that Glenda Jackson thoroughly enjoys her career—with all its agonies—by the degree of commitment she exhibits to her art. Surely the satisfactions must to some extent compensate for the difficulties? On this subject Glenda is also remarkably unromantic.

'Well, I think the satisfactions are usually conspicuous by their absence. It's very rare that you produce in fact the performance on stage that you have imaginatively run in your head when you read a script, even though the ideal is to match the two.

'I suppose the satisfaction is of knowing that you have given a good performance, by which I mean the play has been properly presented, the audience has responded properly and you've contributed your bit as well as or even better than you'd hoped. But it's a fleeting satisfaction because there's always the next performance tomorrow night, which may be absolutely dreadful and there's no way you can guarantee that it won't be.'

Glenda enjoys working in front of the camera as much as she does on stage, although the satisfactions are quite different because of the way films are made.

'Filming is like a very long, extended performance. When I was first working in films a schedule could run from 12 to 24 weeks, that was the average. Now they average 6 to 10. But even so, you have to hang on to a character for 6 to 10 weeks without playing it completely. You are picking it up and putting it down and finding little bits here and there. The satisfaction is finding it, doing it and moving on to the next thing. It's the immediacy of that that I find so very exciting. There is an incredibly concentrated amount of energy, when you actually come to do a take, from everybody around. They're not necessarily looking at you, but there is a concentration on that small, lit square. There's a great deal of waiting about on film and what you have to learn to do is to hang on to your energy so that when they say, "Right, we're going to do it now," you can immediately reach a performance level and manage to retain it for the number of times it may take.'

Even though she has appeared with great success on television, Glenda doesn't think it compares with the other two media. 'I think television is unsatisfactory in every conceivable way,' she says. 'I just think it's a ghastly medium to act in. Although it's better now because they tend to shoot most plays like films these days.'

Whether it's a part in a film or a play or a television series, now that she is in a position to pick and choose Glenda finds it hard to define what makes her decide to do a role.

'I think I'm less attracted to a part than to either the subject or the actual form of the play or film or whatever. It really does rest on whether it's interesting—if it interests me then I'll do it. And what interests me stems out of what I am and I don't know what that is!' She smiles at this.

Having decided to go ahead, Glenda has no special techniques for thinking herself into a new role. 'I find

Glenda with her co-star George Segal in the film *A Touch of Class*. She gave a delightful light comedy performance

I tend to do all my work at rehearsal really, I'm not one for working at home on my own.'

She confidently dispels the myth that you need a different approach to play a comic as opposed to a serious role—and she has proved it several times by her own performances.

'I don't believe there is a different style for acting comedy, I think that's total rubbish. Acting is acting. But if it's physical, fall-about comedy then that's different, because you actually have to be physically able to do that—which takes a particular kind of rehearsal and preparation. But if it's verbal, in the text as it were, I don't see any difference at all.'

Working in the theatre has its own special problems. Glenda has never had to cope with a long run—which is notorious for inducing mild lunacy—for she hasn't done anything for more than six months. But she has always had trouble with nerves.

'I used to be frightened only the first week of a show. I find now I'm afraid every performance and I think that's something that gets worse. It's something you can do absolutely nothing about, you simply have to accept that before the curtain goes up you wish you were anywhere rather than on that stage.

'The happy thing about it is that the minute the curtain *does* go up, you don't have time for that particular form of self-indulgence!'

One thing that is not cured when the curtain rises is the temptation to laugh when something goes wrong. Although some people are worse than others.

'I'm quite good at not corpsing—not laughing. The thing is for me that if I go, it's virtually impossible for me to stop. I mean, I go on until I cry and it's something I'm very afraid of. I hate it, it's a terrifying sensation.'

Far more serious problems can arise if an actor's relationship with the director is not good. Typically, Glenda has strong views on this subject.

'I think it should be said that good directors are very few and far between, although there are many people who call themselves directors. *Very* good directors you can count on the fingers of one hand!

'The ideal relationship is always one in which you have a director you can trust because any theatrical production is a team effort—it's not simply a pecking order of people being told what to do, although that sometimes does happen, I suppose. But the really good directors want to see what the actors are going to do. The really bad directors are the ones that tell you absolutely what to do.

'I think it should be entirely possible to work without bruising your own or other people's egos. It should be possible, but it hardly ever happens because so many people present their egos before they present anything else. And I personally expect directors to be honest with me and I expect them to accept my being honest with them—but quite often that's not the case.'

Off-stage relationships can be difficult, too, because of the actor's peculiar life-style. Glenda finds that she tends to mix with other theatrical people as a result.

'I do because my working hours are unlike most other peoples'—they are in a sense anti-social. If I am in a film, I'm up at six and not home again until late in the evening because I live miles away from the studios, and they start early usually and continue quite late.

'And if I'm doing a play then I'm going out to work when most people are coming in. I think it's a great mistake to think when you're doing a play that you have your days free and just do two hours work at night. I find that from about mid-day it's work time really.'

Close family relationships can also be difficult to maintain as an actor. For a woman there can be the dilemma between having children and pursuing a career, because work can take you away from home, occupy you for most of the day as well as evening and worry you with economic uncertainty. Glenda considers herself lucky in this context because by the time her son was born, she was being offered work which meant she could afford to pay other people to look after her child at home.

'Obviously I've missed a lot of his growing up,' she admits, 'and you always worry about what possible secret damage you may have done by not being there all the time—but he seems OK, touch wood!'

She feels, however, that for young women just

As the schoolteacher Rose, in the play of that name by Andrew Davies. This successful production had a full house every night of the run

starting in their careers, life could be very complicated.

'I know people who got married straight from drama school and had children, but it's very, very hard. A lot of work is still outside London, and are you going to be able to go up to Nottingham or Sheffield or somewhere and take a baby with you? There may be a company with facilities for looking after small babies, but they're very few and far between, I would think.

'Also, you're going to be working for no money. You're going to be paying someone to look after your child and money in the theatre is still very small really.'

Many celebrities complain that fame, and consequently recognition, can be very aggravating, but this may be because they lead the kind of lives that keep them in the limelight. Glenda doesn't consider this a problem.

'No, it's not annoying, but I think that's partly because I live in England and it is a country in which you can do your work and go home. I'm not a sociable person— I don't go to first nights and I don't wish to be part of that showbizzy razzmatazz rubbish. So it's not really a problem and I can lead what I call a normal life *and* work. And when I've done films in America, then that's in Los Angeles where *everybody's* well-known so nobody bothers with you!'

The acting scene in general is very different in America. Glenda says it's infinitely more ruthless and she explains what she means with a particular example.

'When I was in America with *Marat/Sade* in 1966, I made friends with an actress who was appearing in a play which opened in Philadelphia before it moved to New York. And her husband, who was in New York, went down to the news-stand in Times Square to get the out-of-town paper to read the notices.

'He went straight from that news-stand to the station to bring her home because the notice started with her name. He said, "I knew she was going to be fired because the star wasn't getting the notice."

'And he went up to Philadelphia and she didn't get fired, but the part was changed, cut down and altered so that the "name" person was getting all the attention. And that's how it is there.

'There is very little theatre for people to practise in, even less than here. And I think the major difference with here and in America is that here you can fail and try again. You can't fail very often in America and continue to be taken seriously. Mind you, it's very difficult to be taken seriously as a [stage] actor anyway, I think, because essentially they're film/television oriented.'

America excels at stage musicals and films and yet sometimes feels second rate when it comes to the classical theatre. It is for this reason Glenda Jackson thinks certain British actors are held in such high regard.

'I think it is a strange inferiority complex because America has some of the best actors in the world. What it doesn't have is places for them to work. Americans always use Shakespeare as the great watershed of what constitutes good acting. If you can act in Shakespeare they seem to think you can act in anything. And they think that they can't do Shakespeare, but of course they can.

'But it is a very success-oriented society and that has its advantages too. It is that commitment to success, to brilliance, to being the best you can, which makes their musicals as good as they are when they're good; and which makes the British musicals appalling even when they're supposed to be good. There is still a hangover in England that to be professional is somehow to be not quite nice—there is a strong sense of amateurs being nicest.'

Glenda herself displays 'that commitment to being the best you can,' and it is the challenge of maintaining such a high standard that keeps her acting.

'I never regarded it as a glamorous profession; to me the interest was always the difficulty of it. It's very difficult to act well.It's very difficult to really, truthfully present to an audience—in a way that the audience is not aware that you're presenting—what the author wants them to feel or think. You are, in a way, simply a channel between the author and the audience and that's very difficult. So I was always concerned that I would have the opportunities to work within the most difficult fields, and I've been given that—I've been very fortunate.'

And yet she insists that it doesn't matter how determined you are to succeed, without a certain amount of luck you'll get nowhere.

'It doesn't matter how talented you are or how dedicated you are, if you don't have the luck you will never get the opportunity. I was given several opportunities and I was very fortunate in that way. So I think you need luck, but what you do with it is entirely up to you and the attitude you bring to your work.

'I can't emphasize enough that it is a profession that requires a great deal of discipline. It's *not* a lot of people playing games. It's not particularly fun, it's not particularly amusing—I'm talking now about if you take it seriously, which is not the same thing as taking *yourself* seriously. It demands a great deal of you and you have to be disciplined, you have to be healthy and you have to be ready to work when the opportunity presents itself to you. Forget all the stories you read about the temperamental outbursts of people who go and come back because they're so brilliant. They do it once, but they don't go and come back again!'

Just as Glenda is realistic about the amount of grinding hard work involved in being a successful actor, she keeps stressing the difficulty of finding work at all.

'I wish all young people luck when they start, but I think they should be aware that the percentage of people who even *keep* themselves in the acting business is something like 0.2%. Equity not long ago did a breakdown of what actors earn in a year and it came out to something horrendous like £3 [$7.00] a week. It's a vastly oversubscribed profession in which a lot of people want to act and very few get the opportunity.'

She lists unemployment as being undoubtedly the most disagreeable aspect of the life when you're beginning.

'Anybody can say they're an actor or actress and the only way you really know is when you're doing it. And if people don't get the opportunity to do that, it's terribly painful and frustrating because in a way you don't exist—you're not there.'

Furthermore, she thinks new technology will probably limit the job possibilities to an even greater extent, and she can see a growing trend for actors who do more than act.

'For instance, in America it's not unusual for people to be actor/singer/dancers and it may well be that in this country we may have to spread our abilities over a wider area than we've needed to up until now.'

One hopeful sign that she pinpoints for the future is the increasing number of theatre groups created by actors themselves.

'They put on a show, rent a theatre and do a limited season. In that way actors can begin to control their own destinies a little more. It would be a very good thing if one could begin to pool the experiences actors have had in forming their own companies so that we're not always so totally dependant on somebody else employing us. But that doesn't really

Sarah Bernhardt was as temperamental as a whirlwind, a wilful queen of a woman who suffered from the most terrible stage-fright. Here Glenda as Bernhardt decides to leave the stage after a failure; but she returns to become a world legend

apply to young people when they begin, which will always be painful.'

Although Glenda Jackson has herself become a 'star' and has broken through all the barriers, she seems nevertheless to think that every young actor should fully understand that those barriers are there and that once a degree of success has been achieved, the hard work and effort must continue in order to be a true professional. So forget the glamour and the easy life!

She is equally uncompromising when talking about her own future in the theatre. The fact that she is not content to rest on her past successes but continues to demand the challenge of difficult roles makes her seriously doubt that acting will always satisfy her.

'Oh, it won't when I reach that dearth—any minute now—when there just aren't any decent parts for a woman of my age. There's a terrible slough for women because we're terribly badly served for characters really. If you look at the classics, there's really nothing for a woman after Cleopatra until she's in her mid-sixties. And I can't see me hanging around waiting to play the old ladies!'

Television

4

Television is the most recent addition to an actor's livelihood, but bringing plays into people's drawing-rooms has badly damaged the attraction of live theatre. Why should people bother to go into town and pay for seats when they can have fine casts and fine drama on the box? Well, the truth is that live theatre is a very different experience from passive watching. Theatre is a social event, a sharing with one's fellow creatures. Television tends to separate or even isolate, and like so much today one doesn't know whether it is 'real' or not. Is it really her voice? Is this a repeat of a repeat? Oh! *She* was in that terrible series. . . . By invading people's homes, television has a special privilege, but it *can* be switched off in an instant. Unlike the theatre, there is no captive audience.

The Benefits

For the professional actor T.V. has been an enormous bounty, for it is not only plays that offer work. Chat-shows, compèring, children's programmes, voice-overs, commentaries, and hosting all need actors. Compared with the theatre and its evening performances, television keeps civilized hours, and series or serials offer lengthy and well-paid work, especially in America. The strolling actors of yesteryear could never have imagined that life might be so easy for the player. Imagine being in *Coronation*

BAIRD

Entertainment by Radio is extremely satisfactory: add vision to such programmes, and you have at your command the most wonderful home entertainment that the world has ever known.

The receivers made by BAIRD give television at its best. It costs no more to own a BAIRD Receiver, and a complete service of advice, demonstration and installation is available through many first-class dealers.

Model T.26 is a complete entertainer embodying all that is up-to-date and best in the science of television. An attractive leaflet giving full details of this receiver can be obtained from any BAIRD Appointed Dealer or direct from :—

BAIRD TELEVISION LIMITED
CRYSTAL PALACE
ANERLEY HILL, S.E.19.

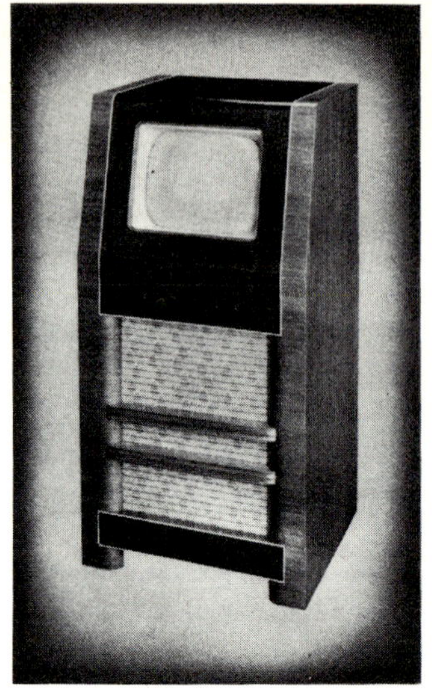

● PRICE 40 GUINEAS ●

PERFECTION BORN OF PATIENT RESEARCH

An early T.V. set; as the advert says: '. . . the most wonderful home entertainment that the world has ever known.' Sadly, T.V. has badly damaged the attraction of cinema and live theatre

America's comedy series *Sanford and Son* was an imitation of the BBC's *Steptoe and Son*. Redd Foxx (standing) and Desmond Wilson took over where Britain's Wilfred Brambell and Harry H. Corbett left off

Street or *Soap*; with a long run, fame and fortune are yours. In fact, it is in television that the actor becomes really well-known, and it can be embarrassing to sit on a bus and be approached by everyone because you were on T.V. last night. You learn to disguise yourself like a spy!

The Drawbacks

A Russian, V. K. Zworkin, and Scotsman John Logie Baird were the scientific pioneers of T.V., and in 1936 Britain put out some pictures from London's Alexandra Palace. America started a public service in 1953 and today, of course, there are many different channels to choose from. T.V. is big business and programmes are bought and sold world-wide. The actor is a commodity, and he must therefore look after his own interests. Perhaps a quarter of all programmes may require actors in some way or other. There is no doubt that television provides a staple pay-packet for many performers. A stage play usually requires a long-term commitment but, unless it is a series, television only takes a short time for each job. A television studio is like a factory. Every day it makes plays, features, comedy programmes, news. Imagine the workshops full of half-constructed sets, the car-parks with high haulage vans, the front reception where every kind of visitor or worker may come through the glass doors, not only actors, but politicians, chauffeurs, or housewives. Imagine, too, the long corridors lined with dressing rooms, the scented make-up chambers, the clothes-packed wardrobes and the studios themselves—high and wide with a cluster of lamps instead of a ceiling, and a prominent clock and stairs leading up to the control rooms.

Plays are rehearsed away from the studios which will be occupied video-taping other programmes. Two or three weeks are spent rehearsing a full-length play, but only a few days for a serial episode. Work is much faster than in the theatre. The director has to find out which of his many cameras will take which shot. Everything he plans must be done without wasting time to meet the tight work schedule of the studios.

For the actor television is like a cross-breed

between the stage and the screen. It is something of both but perhaps more coldly technical than either. Scenes will be continually interrupted in the studio to 'strike' props or furniture so that a camera can creep in between wall and flower-vase. The grand piano might be moved to enable the camera to track backwards as a knot of guests enter the double doors, but when the room is seen fully again, the piano must be back in its place. Some drama directors like to dress rehearse short scenes, and then 'take' them, which means put them on film. Others will attempt to do a whole act without stopping, if it is technically possible. You feel the pressure of time in television, and everyone is conscious that too little time is spent with the cameras. The camera crew may have been doing something entirely different they day before:

filming a baseball game or covering a rock concert.

At worst the actor can be treated like another stick of furniture, because, in the end the director is finally way out of sight up in the control room with his little monitor screens and secretaries and lighting and sound controllers. The actor can be pushed around by remote control! So, it is advisable to remember that eventually it is the actor's performance that will matter most, and of course fine performances *are* seen on television, though not often enough. Actors and actresses are too easily made less effective by this medium. Directors and fellow artists are so often concerned with other pressing matters; no wonder actors sometimes feel that their own judgement of their work is the only worthwhile guide they have.

A scene from BBC T.V.'s *Dr. Jekyll and Mr. Hyde* (1980), with Clive Swift as Dr. Hasty Lanyon (right) and David Hemmings as the doomed Jekyll

5 Jack Mitchell Television Work in Los Angeles

Jack Mitchell has been trying to make a living as a television actor for the last few years. He has appeared in small roles on such series as *The Incredible Hulk*, *Delvecchio*, *Baa Baa Black Sheep*, *Richie Brockelman* and *Quincy* as well as having a regular part in *Paris* as Sergeant Charlie Bogart.

Jack lives in a small house in the more modest part of West Los Angeles with his wife and two children. Inside, the rooms are comfortable with the signs of family life: children's belongings, his wife's painting on an easel, a dog resting under the table away from the hot Californian sun. Outside sits a truck filled with gardening tools—a sign of Jack's 'other profession'. Dressed casually in jeans and a tee-shirt, Jack appears friendly and relaxed, and his natural humour is never far away as he talks about his work.

His life in Los Angeles— like that of so many other aspiring actors— has been frustrating and difficult at times. But at thirty-one years of age he still has high hopes of becoming successful.

Would-be T.V. stars have to live in Los Angeles because that's where most of the American television shows are made—apart from a few exceptions like *Kojak*, which is shot in New York, and *Hawaii Five-0* in Hawaii.

Jack didn't come to L.A. unprepared for his chosen career. In fact he had spent six years training—including gaining a B.A. from the University of

Washington on their Professional Actors' Training Program, and a Masters degree from the California Institute of the Arts. Despite these qualifications work proved very hard to get, especially without an agent.

'Once you have an agent the agent takes care of most of the business, all you generally do is show up. But finding an agent is probably the most difficult part of the business,' he explains.

'The only way you can become aware of what parts there *are* is through an agent. They have "series breakdowns"—a list of all the characters that are going to be in each episode of a given series. Your agent looks through them in case any client of his is appropriate for any particular part and then he will call the casting director.

Jack Mitchell

'Those breakdown sheets are only available to agents. So as an actor, if you don't know any casting people, it is virtually impossible to get a part because you don't know what is available.'

Jack Mitchell is fending for himself on this score since parting company with his agent, and he has managed to find work through contacts in casting departments.

'I think one of the primary ways that people in Los Angeles in films and television get work is by knowing someone. The social scene plays a big, big part in who works and who doesn't.

'I became acquainted with a couple of casting people, so what I do is let them know that I am available and ask if there's anything coming up that I might be right for.'

Having found out what parts there are, the next thing, of course, is to audition for them. Jack says the most nerve-racking part of this is the first reading. After that he relaxes.

'For a good part I think that they certainly have the right to see fifteen or twenty people and pick the best one. But for the two-and-three-line parts it's really difficult for the actor, because there is no acting you can do. What they are really doing is seeing you—checking your teeth, checking your hair. "Yeah, this one's OK, thank you, goodbye!"'

He also points out that it's very difficult to read small parts because often they don't have a point to make, but simply get a more important character from A to B in the story.

'Wonder Woman has to find out where "they" are, so she stops at a gas station and the guy happens to have seen them—"they went thataway" . . . So there is nothing much that you can do with it.'

As a result Jack likes it when you are given a larger part to read to see what you can do, even though the audition is for a much smaller one. However the audition is conducted, the chances of landing the job are still small.

'I would say that when I had an agent, I would go on eight to ten interviews to get one job,' he estimates. 'Without an agent, the chances oddly enough are better because I am only asked to read for parts where someone knows my work. So while I don't have near the number of readings, my chances are better.'

After the audition, you're generally notified as to whether you've got the part the following day, which is three to four days before shooting. Then you are sent the script. Jack describes in detail what happens from that point:

'What I try to do first is just get a general feeling for the episode that I'm doing. I then learn my lines by reading the scenes over and over again and playing them in different ways, trying to get as many different angles on the character as I can. This is really difficult when you have a small part because there are usually not many angles to get.

'Then twenty-four hours before you work, they call you and say be at the studio for make up at six o'clock in the morning and we'll shoot at seven-thirty. They also tell you in advance any particulars you will need to know—if you need to have your hair cut or if you need to shave—and then you go in in the morning.

'You'll meet the first assistant director, who introduces you to the director. Then the first assistant director will take you to your dressing room. You change into your wardrobe and I generally sit and go over my script again. Then the assistant director will introduce you to the other characters whom you're to play the scene with.

'The director then says he would like to rehearse and you stand wherever you are comfortable and read the scene. He then says, "This is what we are going to do. We will have the camera here. We are going to start with you, Jim, over here; and you, Joe, over here. I would like you to cross at some point and get a cup of coffee, Joe; and Jim, when you get to point A take a seat behind the desk and light a cigarette." Then you run through it and the comments are generally confined to "When you light your cigarette, light it with your left hand. Let's see it again." So you walk through it again.

'Then they call "second team", or stand-ins. The stand-ins come in and you go back to your dressing room and they light the scene. It takes anywhere from fifteen minutes to an hour and a half to light a particular shot, and this is the time that I find most effective to rehearse with the other actors. You can get together and work it as you would a stage piece.

Jack Mitchell with outstanding actor James Earl Jones in the television 'police' series *Paris*

'Then they call you back and shoot the scene. The director says, "Action" and away you go. You are usually allowed to finish unless there is some monumental line mess-up. And after you have finished the director says "Cut" and he will talk to you there about the things he wants. He could have told you an hour ago so you would know what he wanted, but that doesn't happen.

'And then you go through the scene again and they shoot it until they like it, which in T.V. is usually three to five times and in films ten to twenty times. Then you are dismissed. You shake hands with the other actors and never see them again. It's very strange, very impersonal.'

Jack says that if you have a good relationship with

the director and you have some ideas of how to get more out of your scene, he will listen and give you a chance. But on the whole Jack thinks acting small parts is very unsatisfactory work.

'You are generally asked to do very little in terms of acting. If I give a strong performance in one particular area and someone else in the scene has worked out a strong performance in another direction, since we only have two rehearsals, there is no time for the director to bring them together; both people look bad, the director doesn't like what he sees and nobody is happy.

'So they would rather have it neutral, they would rather have everything done on an everyday level just like you would talk to somebody who comes to your door. They will make what you say important by moving the camera in, or unimportant by moving the camera back. They will try to do it without the acting if it is at all possible.'

Yet Jack readily admits that the financial rewards of working on television are enormous and can liberate an actor so that he can actually afford to do what he wants professionally.

'If you should happen to land a regular role on a series that runs for four years, you're pretty much set up. You make a lot of money, more money than you could make in ten years of theatre. But other than that, as an actor you are considered in the lowest echelon of the business.'

Originally Jack felt less comfortable working in the theatre. Now he would like to do more stage work, but says there are few opportunities in L.A. except for unpaid work, which he can't afford to do with his family responsibilities.

He would also like to move into films where he feels the standards are higher than in television because there is more time.

'The scripts are generally better in that they are only writing one episode, as it were, on any particular subject. Writers have had time to hone it down and to work it through to where everybody's part means something to a greater degree [than in T.V.]. Also the director is expected to shoot three written pages a day. In television films you are expected to shoot eight to fifteen pages a day. So when you are working in film there is more time for experimentation on everybody's part.'

Jack believes that people with the greatest understanding of human nature make the best actors. But he says that you need more luck than talent to get started in television.

'There are a lot of television actors who can't act. Put them on a stage in front of a lot of people and chances are they would just blend right into the woodwork!

'My guess is that the lucky ones make it in T.V. and the talented ones who've been lucky become stars.'

So far Jack himself hasn't been lucky enough, so he has to do other work—in his case gardening which he likes because it keeps him outdoors—when he's 'resting'.He maintains that you need another activity anyway or you'd go mad.

'It is really important if you are working in television or in films to have something else that you do, because the work you get is so limited in terms of time spent with it—even if you work a lot you're not working very often. A person who gets ten to fifteen parts a year is working a lot, but that may only be forty working days.'

He adds that a lot of people spend their spare time socializing in order to make the right contacts and get more work.

'There is a tremendous amount of casting done on tennis courts, so a lot of people spend their time brushing up on their tennis game!'

If he had his time over again, Jack would prepare himself better for the out-of-work periods.

'I would try not to fall into acting as an only profession as much as I have, because I think it is one of the great roller-coaster professions of all time—you're either up or down. I would try to train myself academically for a sideline that was more lucrative. For example, I think that I probably would try to get a teaching credential so that I could teach high school or a junior high school when I wasn't working.'

Nevertheless Jack is certain of the way you should go about getting into the T.V. business, even though he himself is finding it a struggle.

'If you are interested in doing television work, then you had either better try to establish yourself as a stage actor first and get yourself seen as a stage actor, or you'd better be prepared to do the necessary socializing and political groundwork that you will need to get yourself into some decent roles.'

He also stresses the importance of good training.

'I think that the reason that I have been able to make the beginnings of a career in television is that I had studied for six years and I knew a little about breaking down the script, I had an idea of what to look for in terms of character traits, and how to get a feeling from the written material what character elements the producers and writers felt were important. So I had the training to make the most of the opportunity that I was given. I wasn't given the opportunity because I had the training; but because I had the training I could capitalize on the opportunity.'

Two actors who 'made it' in television: Paul Michael Glaser (left) and David Soul, stars of the popular *Starsky and Hutch*, relaxing on the set

He suggests that you choose a school with as broad a base of acting styles as possible in order to learn more than one method. And the best way of finding out how a particular school works is to go to some of their stage productions and see for yourself. He stresses that once you have learned sound acting, voice and movement principles, you've got something solid to build on.

It is even more difficult for women to find work on T.V. because there are far fewer roles for them.

'Also, there are only three or four different archetypal women in television, and if you're not one of them you are not going to work, unless you're a character actress.

'The studios claim that the reason there aren't more women in television is because they [the studios] are responding to public pressure, and if they put more women in the show, people stop watching—and they give you figures to prove that.'

Despite all the problems, Jack Mitchell keeps going, hoping for the breaks. But he has imposed limits on how long he can keep hoping.

'I think a tremendous amount of it has to do with chance and so the older I get, the more I try to broaden my options in terms of: what would I do if I don't get there? Am I going to be fifty years old, seventy years old, playing the type of parts I'm playing now?

'The answer is no. I have decided that I will continue in this vein for a designated period of time. For me it's about five years— and if in any five-year period there is no progress, then I will have to seriously re-assess my involvement in films and television.'

It is obviously just as hard—if in different ways—to become a television actor as it is to make it in the theatre or films. The Hollywood fairytale of being discovered and becoming an overnight success is far away from the truth. But to Jack Mitchell and others like him, his art inspires him to carry on.

He concludes: 'Acting is rewarding to me in so far as I am able to communicate to the audience something about human nature through the character. That's what got me into acting and that's what keeps me in acting.'

Radio

6

When television was made widely available to the public in the 1950s it hit the well-established business of radio as hard as sound had hit the silent screen. Generations of actors, comedians and radio-journalists had built nation-wide reputations on the radio. They were as familiar a part of people's lives as the 'wireless' itself and the chintz-covered corner chair in the front parlour. Bob Hope and Ed Murrow were as famous in America as Tommy Handley, Alvar Liddell and, later, the Goons were in Britain. Inevitably, when television arrived offering pictures as well as sound, radio was relegated to second place as a home entertainment: a private, personal pleasure for those who delight in music or rich verbal drama.

Britain didn't entrust the powerful medium of radio to private and perhaps irresponsible hands. In 1927 the BBC (British Broadcasting Corporation) was formed as a 'public service' for which listeners paid a small licence fee. America let big business into its radio and for some time there were hundreds of small companies jingling their advertisements between variety acts and musical offerings. Eventually, four large networks were formed: MBS, CBS, NBC and ABC.

In England, radio acting is still an important part of an actor's life. The BBC keeps a small repertory company of players, and other actors are recruited

During World War II radio was a vital means of communication, providing news, features and variety entertainment. Here a BBC engineer prepares to send out the programme 'A London Letter' to North America. Behind him Macdonald Hastings is ready to speak

from time to time. A good deal of drama is broadcast weekly, as well as one or two daily serials (some of which have been running for twenty years or more). Lately, commercial radio has plunged into drama too, but hearing classic plays chopped into melodramatic quarters of an hour with advertisements inserted between is a different thing from listening undisturbed for an hour or more and truly entering into the world of the play.

We've noted that the mask can 'release' an actor's powers, and so can radio because it doesn't involve physical presentation. Just as the listener's imagination is freed by radio (if you cannot *see* what a room looks like you can imagine it any way you like), so the actor is in no way inhibited by his appearance or his character's appearance. All is in the voice. The character is in sound only. Clearly the vocally versatile actor does well in radio and it doesn't matter whether he looks right for the role or not. Elderly ladies can play Juliet and fat men can play romantic leads. From start to finish you hold the script in your hand; this means that work can be done very quickly. As long as you can read well and can make the part come alive you will enjoy radio work. VHF and stereo have added to the quality of radio

This team practised for two weeks in order to make convincing sound effects for H. G. Wells' eerie *War of the Worlds* in 1951. When Orson Welles told the story in America, thousands of radio listeners thought the broadcast was real and panicked because Martians were invading Earth!

sound and recently there have been experiments with binaural sound: sounds built up in layers as they are in real life— a voice close-by, someone else in the kitchen behind, a car passing down the street outside—all at the same time, graded into different levels.

Britain has a proud record of radio writing. Tom Stoppard and Harold Pinter both began in radio, and Dylan Thomas's *Under Milk Wood* was acclaimed as a richly evocative radio poem. Speech and speaking are the basis of a radio actor's art. Therefore as a radio performer you must be concerned with the words and the thoughts you convey with your voice, not merely your vocal skills. You must certainly be careful not to fall in love with the sound of your own voice!

Sound effects are important, however, and they are done by a studio assistant laden with 'props': pages to rustle, drinks to pour, doors to knock. The studios are acoustically designed to create different indoor and outdoor 'atmospheres', and even though you are only in front of a set of microphones, you can work up exciting dramatic relationships with your fellow actors. Some directors favour doing plays on location. They take the players and scripts and microphones on to city rooftops or into a country garden and they do the play there. It is usually very helpful because the actor no longer has to remember to imagine his surroundings. But there are limitations to location radio. Money wouldn't be available to set up a full nineteenth-century ballroom scene, dancing couples, orchestra and all. You might as well put the whole thing on film!

Radio drama is, inevitably, a minority entertainment, and radio is perhaps most valuable as a living storehouse of lesser known fiction and classical drama. In the theatre minor works cannot be given major productions—it is too expensive. But they *can* be beautifully produced on radio.

The spoken word is the real treasure of radio. No medium is better suited to show us the constant

changes in our speech and the growth of our own language. Perhaps it is verbal comedy that comes off best. Think how so much radio comedy surprises us with its surrealistic invention, its crazy non-sequiturs and its joining together of dissimilar ideas. Radio stimulates the mind, through the ear.

Great intimacy can be achieved on radio. Just listen to one of Alistair Cooke's *Letters From America* given in the style of a personal chat to a friend. At the BBC in London the recital pianists are even asked to play 'as though to one person'.

To illustrate the work a radio actor does, here is an extract from *Hector's Fixed Idea* by Bruce Stewart, a play about Hector Berlioz, the composer. We can see what the actors have to do and how they must fit in to the whole design. Sound effects are as important as

Three of the famous Goons: Harry Secombe (left), Spike Milligan—with a new nose—and Peter Sellers. Wisely the fourth member of the crazy quartet, Michael Bentine, is nowhere to be seen!

talk. Berlioz is planning to kill his lady-love's fiancé. He's mad with jealousy and has bought pistols for the duel. He has decided to travel disguised as a woman.

PAGE 29

(COACH AND HORSES PULL UP WITH A JERK)

1. BERLIOZ: (*little gasp*) Why have we stopped?

2. LADY: It is a Customs Post, Madame.

3. BERLIOZ: Why can't we push on?

(COACH DOOR OPENED)

4. CICCO: Buona sera, Signori, Signore. Permit me to assist you to alight, Signora.

5. BERLIOZ: I do not desire to alight, Captain. I merely want to stretch my crushed limbs. . . .

(CLATTER AS PISTOLS DROP TO THE FLOOR)

6. LADY: (*a squeak*) Pistols! From under her skirts—pistols! To think I've travelled all these miles with something in skirts that is not a woman . . .

7. CICCO: Signora, do not faint.

8. BERLIOZ: (*moving away*) Oh! let me out of this . . .

9. CICCO: Come back!

10. BERLIOZ: (*off*) No!

11. CICCO: Halt or I fire! You hear me spy? Ciccolini, crack shot of the Customs service will fire . . .

(PISTOL SHOTS. THE LADY SCREAMS. CONFUSION.

BRING UP MUSIC WHICH DROWNS OUT EFFECT.

PAUSE.

FADE UP VOICES. SMALL GROUP IN CUSTOMS ROOM.)

12. CICCO: So. M'sieur, we will go over the matter again. Ciccolini will probe to the truth at last.

13. BERLIOZ: (*weary*) Oh! please, haven't we gone over it quite enough now?

The numbers down the left hand side make it easy for the studio to refer instantly to the same place at once. 'Page 29, Speech 10', says the director, and all look there. 'Berlioz, go farther off on that speech, you were still too close. You sounded as though you were still in the carriage.' 'Fine', says the actor playing Berlioz.

The whole script is laid out carefully so the eye sees immediately what is talk and what are stage directions or sound effects. This is very helpful to the actor when he's actually performing.

Often the actor will have to wait for a cue light before speaking, even in the middle of a scene when he's pent up with emotion. If he doesn't, then the carriage might not have stopped in the right place, or the pistols might not have fired before someone shrieks. Some effects—for instance the dropping of the pistols from Berlioz's skirt—will be done by an assistant standing alongside the actor, because the same sound acoustic must be achieved as when the actors are talking. Otherwise the pistols won't sound as though they have literally dropped at his feet. But the coach and horses stopping and the music, when it 'wipes' the scene, will be done from the control panel, separate from the studio floor.

Obviously it would be best to begin the second scene by fading up Ciccolini's voice gradually (Bruce Stewart says this in his play). Thus the audience 'enter' the room.

If you were playing Hector Berlioz you would have to sound like a woman to begin with, and then, when the pistols fell, perhaps your voice would break with the shock. That's why the Lady can instantly say: 'To think I've travelled with something in skirts that is not a woman.'

So you can see that radio is fun and is work that needs a lot of concentration. The actor must always have a cool mind controlling everything he does.

7 Sara Coward
Acting in Radio and Rep

Sara Coward lives in a bright attic flat high above the noise of a busy road in north London. Walking barefoot round the room in a long summer dress, she is strikingly tanned and at ease after a short holiday abroad. Her manner is warm and vivacious, with an occasional flash of toughness underneath as she speaks seriously of her life and her job.

Sara is an actress who actually works regularly. Although she's not—yet—a household name or superstar, in an overcrowded and highly competitive profession she is doing reasonably well.

Sara started acting at school and decided when she was sixteen that she'd like to make it her career. However, she was doing very well academically and her parents and teachers wanted her to go to university—possibly Oxford—to read English. When she discovered that a few universities did a drama degree course, she applied to the one with the best reputation, which was Bristol (they only took one per cent of the applicants). This, she felt, was a good compromise, for her parents were completely against her going to drama school.

'They made it very clear that they didn't want me to become an actress because it had no security—they wanted me to do something worthwhile like teaching,' she explains.

But ultimately her parents were pleased that she was accepted at Bristol because they knew how hard

Sara Coward says this is the only photograph of herself that has brought her work

it was to get in.

She enjoyed her three years there, 'but as a city Bristol was too slow moving for me as I had been brought up in London. So after I graduated I applied to London drama schools instead of the Bristol Old Vic School.'

As she had already had a grant for three years (you usually only get four years on a grant in the UK) she only had one year left and most of the courses ran for three years. However, the Guildhall School at that time ran a two-year course which she was invited to join for the second year.

'I knew that the last year meant that you got seen by agents because they have "shopwindow" productions then, so I took the place. But it is very difficult to walk into the last year because it is hard to start from scratch in voice and movement lessons when everyone else is twelve months ahead.

'I found it very boring at drama school,' Sara admits. 'I was twenty-one when I went, not fifteen or sixteen, and they wasted so much time between classes doing nothing.'

Yet she was pleased when she won the Radio Scholarship for her year.

'I thought, well OK, at least I've got a job to go to and a union card, and even then (I think it's worse now) a union card was difficult to get.'

Every year the BBC Drama Repertory Company takes only one male and one female student, so it's obviously very difficult to get in. Once contracted to the company, however, you're paid a weekly salary which gives a kind of security not often found in the acting world. Although in many ways it was a great start for Sara, she found it frustrating.

'At that time they had too many women in the company so I wasn't used that much. I would be used by two or three producers who liked my work a great deal, otherwise I would be used to fill in waitresses, bus conductresses—the three-line things. It was very boring.

'And all I wanted to do was theatre. I wanted to see people in front of me, not a microphone.'

Sara's wish was soon granted—just before her contract ran out she auditioned for a small theatre company in St Andrew's, Scotland and was asked to join. There were only three men and three women and they were all getting the same tiny wage—including the director. But she enjoyed her six months there and felt they did some good work, including some commercial plays during the tourist season.

She left the company to have her tonsils out and then returned to London. After that, apart from a small television part, she didn't work again for four or five months.

'You think: I shall never work again. I'm just rubbish, nobody wants me. I've had my tonsils out and I can't talk anymore and I'm useless.'

Then suddenly she was offered both the understudy of a leading part in the West End of London and the 'female juvenile' part in a weekly repertory company in Guernsey.

'And I thought: what do I do? Do I stick in the West End and be safe again like I was in radio, or do I go out to the provinces and play for virtually nothing and get the experience?'

Sara decided on the latter course and played all sorts of parts. She had to learn new roles quickly because the company did a different play every week, and soon she instinctively knew how to 'handle' an audience.

Once back in London again with nothing much happening, Sara and another actress, Jo Anderson, decided to start their own company. They wrote and produced a show about Newgate prison in the eighteenth century.

'It was extraordinary being on the other side of the fence—being the employer for once. We used to see some dreadful actors at auditions—you can tell very quickly if an actor's good or bad.'

They played the show in various places, ending up doing two weeks at the Bush Theatre in London where they were reviewed by the big national newspapers, which was good publicity.

They got together for a series of productions after that, whenever both of them were out of work at the same time. They only just about covered their costs though, and the actors rehearsed for nothing because they liked what they were doing.

Meanwhile Sara was doing a lot of rep work—six months here or there or a tour. At the Chichester Festival she had a lucky break. She was understudy in the Prospect Theatre Company's production of *A Month In The Country* and was spotted by Timothy West (star actor and a director of the company) at a rehearsal. This led to her getting a small part (Katya) and understudying the role of Vera again when the Prospect re-did the play later on. And this time she actually got to play Vera in London for the last twelve weeks of the run once the original actress had dropped out.

Back in rep with various companies, Sara played major roles in *Cabaret*, *Macbeth* and many other productions, albeit out of London.

With her own company she did a show called *Ludwig*, written by Jo Anderson, about the life of Beethoven. Sara played all his mistresses as well as his sister-in-law, and she thoroughly enjoyed it.

'I love being able to change from one part to another in front of an audience,' she says. 'We did two weeks at the Roundhouse in London, which was nice.

Sara as Katya in the Prospect Theatre Company's production of *A Month in the Country*

But I was beginning to get disenchanted with the idea of our own company because the people we really wanted couldn't afford to work for us.'

Then she landed the parts of Marianne Faithfull, Bianca Jagger and six other women in a show called *Let The Good Stones Roll* which was to be performed at the Edinburgh Festival.

'It was a young company, a with-it company and a good company. It was a great success on the Fringe and it got one of the best write-ups that year,' she recalls.

Six months later it was decided to produce it in the West End and Sara was asked to play the same parts. But this time it had to be lengthened from a one-acter to a full length play.

'The script didn't take the weight,' she confesses. 'We took it to Newcastle for the pre-London run and re-wrote it a lot, took numbers out, put numbers in. At that point, had the show been successful, the guy who played Mick Jagger and I could be stars now because the newspapers were all rivetted by the idea of doing a musical about the Rolling Stones. In fact, somebody blew our publicity too soon. The big nationals did all their stuff and I made the front page of one of them. And then we brought the show to London and we were in the amazing position of having all the publicity we wanted and knowing the product wasn't up to it— and they slated it. So what did I do? I went back to rep,' she laughs.

Sara is very much back in radio, too, these days. She plays Caroline in *The Archers*—a radio soap opera which has been running for thirty years and is practically a British institution. It is broadcast twice daily and concerns the everyday life of an English farming community.

'There is no running contract,' explains Sara, 'you are employed per episode. It is completely luck whether the writer wants to write for you that week.

'I am not a real radio actress. A radio actor is something quite apart—they can produce the goods *immediately*. But for me it's half working because they can't see you.

'Now a real radio actor would tell you that because they can't see you, you have complete freedom. You're not tied down by your looks, your personality, your age or anything else. You can do anything with your voice, you can give them any image you want to. It's the only medium in which the audience has complete freedom to imagine what's going on—a good radio play can be magic for that reason.

'It is a specialized medium which is not *my* speciality but which I can do. But I don't think I'm *very* good at it and yet that's how I make my living, which is sad.'

The Archers is recorded for two-and-a-half solid days twice a month (an episode lasts fifteen minutes). The cast reads through a whole episode once and then rehearses, so it takes about two hours to do a fifteen-minute recording. They use a lot of sound effects, of course, and have six microphones in the studio, each with a different atmosphere to create the pub, the open air, the stables etc.

The actors receive the script about a week in advance, but they don't have to memorize the lines—simply learn how to turn the script pages silently!

Sara has been in *The Archers* for over eighteen

months now although she was originally intended only to be a 'county' girl who comes to the village for six to twelve weeks. But compared with some of the veteran characters she's still a newcomer!

Sometimes she gets letters addressed to Caroline 'which is a bit difficult,' she admits. 'I will reply as myself, almost assuming the character exists. "It is awfully kind of you to ask about Caroline's horse. In fact he was last seen with so-and-so and he broke his leg, and oh, how dreadful!" I'll be a bit funny about it, but almost talk about the character as if she were a separate person that I know. It's a weird, weird feeling.'

Sara thinks that working in T.V. is the only way to make a name for yourself at the moment in Britain. 'Films are about dead. Theatre—you can do wonderful work but who gets to see it? The only way you can get respect and standing is by doing television. And I can't get to do that, which is my big frustration.'

Although she got some T.V. work through somebody she knew, she says that it is so difficult to get into television because people don't take chances by using unknown or untested actors.

'They don't dare because they are in such a precarious position. The BBC have cut down on the number of contract directors, therefore most people are freelance and, like actors, are employed by the results of their last job—if they didn't get the ratings then they're finished.'

Even though she claims that you need T.V. to get known, Sara would choose the theatre every time for satisfaction.

'It's very nice to be recognized, but it's not important. For me what is important is being respected for the work you produce.'

In her view women have a tougher time in the theatre because 'in the end the ingredients of a play are more men than women, unless you are talking about some very specialized feminist play, which I don't believe in because it's false.'

Also, women are more stereotyped than men: 'It's very difficult unless you are very, very pretty, like chocolate box pretty, or you are a character actress, which means you've got a large nose or you're too fat, because then they know where to put you.'

Sara surrounded by fans of *The Archers* at the studios where the programme is produced

Although there are more women competing for fewer jobs than men, both ultimately face the same problems of finding work at all. Sara got a secretarial qualification 'so that if I'm absolutely broke, I needn't go on the dole [welfare]; I can say I'm an agency typist.'

Drama school does not prepare you for this situation, she says.

'They teach you how to act, how to talk, how to move but they don't teach you how to survive, to exist when there is nothing else to prop you up. I feel very strongly that at every acting school the classes in the final year—or even in the first year—should be taken down to the dole and shown what it's like to sign on for the first time.

'That's where we belong when we're out of work. It's a privilege to work in this profession and we should be reminded of it at all times.'

Sara says that above all you need luck to succeed. Plus 'a gift which is more valuable than talent in the acting profession—the ability to "sell" yourself—if you can walk into an interview or write a letter which will sell you, which will make them think, "I've got to see this person," then your chances are greatly improved.'

She also thinks that having attended a drama school with a good reputation can help you on your way by its name alone, although whether you actually learn anything or not depends on the individual teachers, 'and they could be rubbish working at a wonderful school, or absolutely wonderful working at a place with no name at all!'

Yet she insists that you should go ahead and try if you really want to act, 'but realize that it is going to ruin your ideals, break your heart and kill you financially.'

So to persevere under such gloomy conditions, as Sara has, you need to have a great deal of confidence in your abilities.

'I stay in it because I know I'm good and I think that maybe one day the rest of the world might accept that too.'

She obviously also derives a particular kind of satisfaction from her work that nothing else could supply.

'I want to be stretched,' she explains, 'to work and get excitement out of it. I'm not talking about the glamour of the first night or anything like that. It's the spark that happens between people on stage doing a good play. *That's* what it's all about. And the memory of it keeps you going from job to job.'

Amateur

8

Acting is natural. You may have heard someone say about a professional performer 'Oh! he's a natural.' What they mean is that the person can act by instinct; perhaps he has no need to go to a drama school. Surprisingly everyone can act a little. Just think of how much we learn and grow by imitating what we see around us; and imitation is a kind of acting isn't it? We're all born with the ability to copy. In our early years we take and adapt many mannerisms and characteristics from our family. Unconsciously we borrow ways of talking or even walking from those we admire. And, of course, we learn to do many things by literally copying from someone else. We look and we imitate.

At School

It isn't surprising that many children want to act at school, and that so many schools include drama as part of their curriculum. Theatre in education has come to play an important part in teaching methods, and acting out situations proves a classroom favourite. In this way people are physically involved in doing something as opposed to sitting at their desks, and role-playing (taking a part) is the best way to know what it feels like to be a particular person in a particular situation. The learned judge has to make difficult decisions, the crook shivers and shakes in the witness box and the clever lawyer has to use all

A cast photo from a school production of Shakespeare's *King Henry IV*. The Wardrobe Supervisor has found excellent costumes and the cast incorporates the entire age-range of the school

his brains and power of speech in order to defend his client. As soon as we pretend to be these people we understand the whole business of trial (and error!) completely.

Many schools are visited by professional troupes and usually invited to take part in discussion after the show; or it may be that the session has been designed to let the children perform. So much the better. Most of us, if we can overcome our shyness, like taking the stage.

Play Readings

If you want to continue this kind of activity in vacation-time or after you've finished with school there are many ways and opportunities to do so. Have you ever thought of just reading plays, of getting a few copies of a famous or 'hit' play from the library and, having read it through in private once or twice, getting together with six or eight friends and acting it out? Don't worry about moving as though it were on a stage, just read. Put your heart and soul into your part. Mean what you say. You'll be amazed at how funny or exciting it can be, and this is what professional actors do after they have been cast in a play. They read and re-read and re-read. Every time—if the play is any good—they will gather more information about the characters and how to act the play. Plays are not novels; they haven't been written to be read silently. They've been written with an audience in mind. It is always the playwright's intention to engage the interest (and if possible the laughter and tears) of an audience. Remember that when you read aloud. Show off. Do whatever you think your character should be doing and remember that *action* is the life of a play. Even with scripts that seem lifeless, where people just go on talking for what seems like hours on end, *something will be happening*, and probably something important. Ibsen's *The Doll's House* works up to a moment of great action, at the very end. Nora, the heroine, walks out on her husband. From the moment the play has begun that is what the playwright is working towards. Always think what your character would be physically doing: ironing, making cakes, reading, writing a letter. There will come moments of inspiration when you know that your character has to be doing a particular action, to make the scene just right. These moments of creation are a delight, for they are when an actor contributes importantly to a piece of theatre.

All groups must have some kind of leader or leaders. In play readings unless someone is prepared to arrange the meeting place and the refreshments during the course of the sessions, and to oversee the collecting and returning of copies, the group won't run smoothly and people will lose interest. Certainly play reading is great fun and by coming into contact with some good plays your own original work will benefit. You'll also improve your vocabulary and get to know many things you didn't know before. Actors constantly learn new things from the wide variety of parts they play.

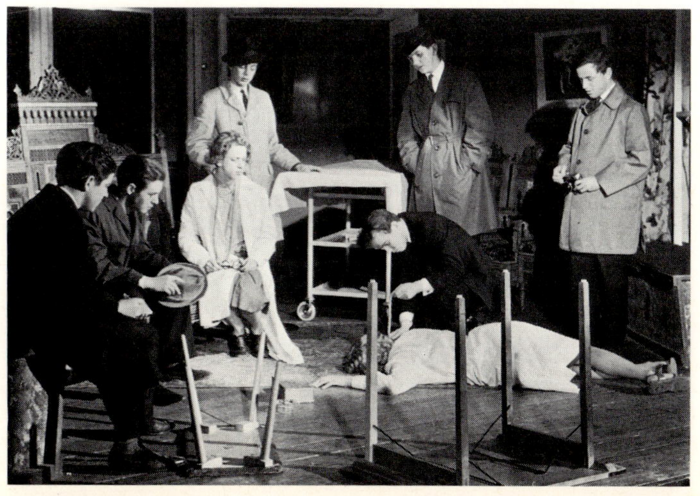

A school performance of Friedrich Durrenmatt's play *The Physicists*. By looking at the players' faces and body positions you can see that everyone is acting well

College

College or university is the next step on the road for many of us, and of course most places of higher education have flourishing drama societies and perhaps their own theatre. In England if you are very keen there is usually some kind of job to be done around a college theatre, even if it is only joining in the chorus or sweeping the stage. The university drama department will probably make full use of its theatre, for many of the undergraduates will be thinking about turning professional; not only as actors but as teachers, directors or drama critics. Many American universities have fine theatre arts departments that offer intensive drama training at both the undergraduate and graduate level. Their theatres are often better designed, with far more modern technical equipment, than the professional theatres outside!

Community Theatre—Britain and America

Even if you do not attend university, there is a whole world of amateur and community theatre open to you, though there is a marked difference between the amateur movement in Britain and America. The British do theirs mostly for fun, while the American community theatres are very nearly professional in their outlook and sense of purpose.

The founders of the famous Abbey Theatre in Dublin, Ireland, first showed many amateurs that their theatre could have a serious purpose. The poet Yeats and his patron and friend Lady Gregory were 'amateurs' who formed a small circle of workers to establish a genuine 'people's theatre'. This was just at the turn of the twentieth century. As a result the 'Abbey' was founded. By 'people's theatre' Lady Gregory meant a place where drama about ordinary people and their lives could be shown, and where those very people could feel free to involve themselves in what was going on. Ireland (Eire) has a turbulent history and the Abbey Theatre has often reflected this in the content of its plays. In 1926 there was a public riot at the first night of Sean O'Casey's play *The Plough and the Stars*, a drama about the Easter Rising of 1916 when Irish Republicans rebelled against their English masters. To this day the

The original Abbey Theatre in Dublin which was destroyed by fire in 1951. A smart new theatre now stands on the site. The first Abbey players were amateurs

Abbey remains a successful playhouse committed to drama that portrays relevant social issues.

The Abbey showed what community theatre, and indeed all theatre, could be: a place to stir public debate. Of course, there must also be room for diverting spectacle. Plays have to be enjoyable as well as instructive; every good playwright knows that. Since audiences tend to prefer the easy stuff that won't be too disturbing, entertainment will always be an important function of the theatre.

In the United States community theatres were built in areas where few professionals came. Very often the local people put up their theatre themselves and certainly they always clubbed together to raise the money. Often it is the locals who act, manage and direct, but in many places professionals of some kind or other are used on the staff, either as performers and directors or as administrators and backstage personnel. There are more than two thousand community theatres of one kind or another, in the mean streets of depressed cities or in open country amidst the golf courses and country clubs. The headquarters of the American Theater Association (to which the Association of Community Theaters is affiliated) is in Washington, D.C. There you can get advice of any sort, from how to start a small group to where to hire a theatre director for a near six-figure

An amateur actor gets to work with his stick of greasepaint to make up for the role of Curley in *Oklahoma*

salary. Through this Association community theatres have tried to assemble their long experience for the benefit of the movement as a whole. The idea is an exciting one and without such an organization many areas in America would be without theatre and therefore without a communal meeting place. Gone are the days when the church was the centre of social life: theatre provides a good substitute.

There is another fascinating side to community theatre: it mixes professional with amateur actors. This cannot happen in Britain; the actors' trade union won't allow it. But as more leisure time comes for more people it seems inevitable that Britain will follow the American pattern, a good thing too, if more people are going to make and enjoy theatre. Somewhere, however, the highest professional standards must be maintained to remind us of what we are trying to achieve.

British amateur and professional theatre are quite separate. The professional and the amateur watch one another warily. The 'pro' thinks the amateur plays at theatre and knows nothing of the hard times and the pressure that can come with long runs and the high expectation of an audience. The amateur envies the pro because he gains the fame and the fortune (occasionally) and spends all day doing what the amateur can only do in his spare time. 'Sure I'd like to go to acting classes and sure I'd like to be on television—but I'm a doctor (or an accountant or a mechanic): how can I?' Well, you can only if you are prepared to take the risk and put your family's security in jeopardy too. It is that element of risk that makes the pro think himself superior to the amateur, combined with the fact that he *has* to think he is more talented. Otherwise he's in the wrong job, isn't he?

British amateurs number perhaps a quarter of a million and play up and down the country in village halls, school assembly rooms and theatres. Organizations such as the National Operatic and Dramatic Association and the British Theatre Association, both based in London, and the Central Council for Amateur Theatre in Banbury, Oxfordshire will help enquirers and explain the work of over 18,000 amateur groups, their contests and their festivals. For instance, the Manchester Athenaeum Dramatic Society was formed in 1847 and is still going strong, and a handful of notable clubs possess their own theatres like the Questors at Ealing, the Bradford Civic (the closest there is to an American community theatre outside the profession), the Norwich Maddermarket and the People's Theatre, Newcastle-upon-Tyne. These societies have strong traditions and it is to be hoped that more like them will come to exist in the future.

The Questors Theatre in Ealing, London was built by amateurs for their own purposes. The 'What's Next' notice-board suggests they are very busy

America is far ahead in the race to build theatres which whole communities can be part of. The blending of professional and amateur is the key to this growth. In Britain, most areas are served by some kind of professional theatre because the island is so small and accessible compared with America. In the States other means of bringing theatre to people must be found and community theatres are the result. However, the professional actor and actress should fully support the amateur movement because it can give them the opportunity to work, albeit for a very low wage, and they, in turn, can pass on some of their special know-how to those they work with. The pro might have a different approach from the amateur: he should be technically much more in command. But the amateur can fire the pro with his enthusiasm and hard work and, as a result, the pro may be forced to drop some of his stale tricks and open his heart up again to the painful and dangerous business of acting. Certainly in physical and vocal

An open-air production of *Pirates of Penzance* at New York's Delacorte Theater in Central Park

preparation, and probably in disciplines like improvisation, a professional performer would be a valuable and welcome member in any community theatre. If the leaders of the community movement in the States see their dreams come true, then their hard work will have brought popular and worthwhile theatre to the length and breadth of the land.

Join!

Many community and amateur theatres have a youth programme, for they know that they must look to the future. The sooner children become familiar with the tricks of the trade (and the essential technical knowledge which is part of modern theatre) the better. Those who think of theatres as friendly and exciting places will want to go there to watch plays too. Ideally, these theatres should be open as much of the day as possible and a wide variety of activities could go on there. There could be a crèche, a restaurant, an exhibition of photographs or paintings in the foyer, music— as many different things as possible. That's the way to attract families to the building, and once inside they are bound to be curious enough to want to see the show. Whether you are on stage or off it, if you love theatre you'll want to involve yourself in some group, somewhere, and help a whole community work towards enjoying and possessing a theatre of its own.

It is surprising that there isn't more state-backed youth theatre available in the U.S. In England Michael Croft has set up a splendid company, the National Youth Theatre of Great Britain, founded in 1956. Every year thousands of youngsters audition for him. Unfortunately, because most plays have far fewer female characters than male, the girls still have less chance of being used than the boys. Michael Croft has taken his company to New York and to Ontario, Canada, and he sees no reason why other large-scale youth theatres cannot be founded. But as yet North America hasn't followed Europe in achieving this. In England, however, there are some community theatres which use young people. Anna Scher of north London and the Common Stock Company at Hammersmith, have both achieved fine reputations for their youth work.

Zigger Zagger by Peter Terson has been one of the National Youth Theatre's happiest successes; but how many girls got parts?

The most famous amateur actors of all are portrayed in Shakespeare's *A Midsummer Night's Dream*. The 'mechanicals', as they are known are 'hard-handed men' (labourers) who try to put on a play for the Duke's wedding. Never has so much effort been made by so ill-suited a bunch to so little effect! They are amazed when their play is chosen. Their hearts beat like butterfly wings. Bully Bottom, their chief actor, makes an ass of himself, and poor young Francis Flute has to dress up as a woman, even though he has 'a beard coming'. Snug, the joiner, trembles even as he roars like a lion, and skinny Starveling loses his temper with the sarcastic courtiers. But at the end the Duke says 'never anything can be amiss when simpleness and duty tender it'. He means that they all tried as hard as they could and did their best out of love and respect. If only all audiences were as forgiving as Shakespeare's Duke of Athens!

Professional

9

Stage Schools

Some stage schools accept children from about the age of ten and include a general education in their syllabus; but school work will be interrupted to do acting jobs that crop up and, often, the school will act as an agent in such circumstances.

In England conditions of work for young people are very strict. Only a limited number of hours or performances are allowed and the children always have to be properly chaperoned. Part of their earnings must be set aside as savings for them. However, auditions or interviews for work are not restricted to students at stage schools: those casting will very often spread their nets open to untrained children as well.

The arguments against sending children to a stage school are the same as those against too early specialization in any subject. It may be that left alone to follow their own inclinations, children will pursue some other path than theatre and finally find their way into different work. Although many children show a very early aptitude for performing it does not necessarily mean that when they are adult they will want to follow the actor's life. They may not thank their parents for channelling them so young into show business. On the other hand, early starts can pay off. Both Mickey Rooney and Sir Richard Attenborough were child stars, and even now they

There are several children in the musical *Annie*. In fact, the leading lady is supposed to be only ten years old

are still at the top of their profession. Certain show-business families assume that their offspring will follow in the parental footsteps; the sooner they get experience, the better. Certainly children will better learn to survive the hurly-burly of auditions and the disappointments of the actor's life at a stage school. They'll also get used to the idea of working hard and of being directed.

In Shakespeare's *Hamlet*, Rosencrantz calls the boy actors 'little eyases' that 'cry out on top of question and are most tyrannically clapped for't'. By 'eyases' Shakespeare meant young hawks that have been stolen from their mother's nest. Stage schools teach their pupils to push for themselves and toughen up to the demanding life that lies ahead.

Acting Schools

The majority of acting schools take students from the age of seventeen, and usually contain quite a blend of ages and backgrounds. This is generally better for the young students than the older ones, and it is the young students we focus on here. The best schools provide a three-year course and teach voice production, singing, text work, improvisation, costume, some history of the theatre and, perhaps, stage management. They will try to provide the student with an approach to his job, a way of working that will give him a life-jacket to put on when the stormy seas of theatre get too rough. Who can know how good a director will be and how helpful to each individual artist? Very often the actor has to look after himself, and so his drama school training must stand him in good stead. Schools, after all, are there to let the student act. Being among contemporaries he will quickly get some idea of his own abilities. Schools will also push the student into playing parts that don't immediately seem right for him. They'll provide the student with a wider experience, in all likelihood, than that which will come his way professionally in the early years. And schools will do all they can to launch their key students into the business with a flourish by arranging a job or an agent.

Drama schools are a mixed bunch and provide no guarantee of professional work. But the best schools do try to give the student a solid basis of technique (acting, dancing and singing), and teach him about some of the realities ahead when he's left to sink or swim in the profession.

Two actors participate in a 'mirror' exercise at the Drama Studio, Ealing—a London drama school. Which one leads? Try it and see

In Britain recently the National Council for Drama Training had a close look at twenty drama schools and give fifteen of them a kind of seal of approval. This caused an uproar because there might be a danger of students from these schools gaining their Equity (union) card, and therefore their entrance to the profession, sooner than other newcomers. For a long time it has been a free-for-all concerning who manages to get his union card and who doesn't, and this is partly because too many mediocre coaches encourage too much mediocre talent. Some standard should apply before a school takes money from students and, after putting them through the course, flings them out into the cold and difficult 'showbiz' world. The profession itself must decide what is the best training for actors, and there is no reason why the best students at the best schools (if these can be judged) should not be among the first to gain entry into the profession. The free-for-all, although it seems democratic, is open to too much abuse. Everyone needs *some* physical and vocal training, no matter how talented they are and no matter how old; but the training must be of real value.

Do everything the hard way. Go to the toughest auditions (eight hundred applicants for twenty-four places) at the best schools. Then you'll really know where you stand. If one of the most respected schools wants you, no doubt you will be determined enough to find some way to finance your training. (If you're lucky you may even get a grant.) There are never any half-measures for those who are truly going to make it; don't *expect* anyone to help you!

Starting Your Career

Once you are out of acting school, life will suddenly seem very empty by comparison. You will no longer have things organized for you, and you will do anything that calls itself Theatre, whether you are paid or not. Most likely you will have to support yourself by taking part-time employment. Your main pre-occupation will be seeking out those who are in a position to give you acting work. You will traipse from agent to agent, from open audition to open audition and you will be glad to take advice and *hope* from anyone. This is where agents come in, men and women whose business it is to put actors and actresses in touch with employment. Agents come in all shapes and sizes, from those with glossy offices and big cigars to those who, like you, are eager to get work from whom they can. You must not choose an agent who is a beginner himself. The greatest asset an agent has is a solid knowledge of showbusiness. He should know far more than you do about where to go for work and who might be likely to employ you. There are many minor jobs an actor can fulfil that can't be called acting: selling things, ushering, modelling, market-research. You must try not to be side-tracked into doing these things that will lessen your chances to perform. You must always try to make yourself free to follow every avenue which might lead to you being given a part, and you must be prepared to go far away, from friends or family. If you hang around Los Angeles or London waiting for a film or a T.V. 'break' you are wasting valuable time during which you might be gaining real acting experience. Ian McKellen, who is now one of Britain's leading actors, insisted upon staying in the provinces until he was ready to take major roles in major productions. The actor has to be an idealist, unless he is prepared to settle for second or third best very early in his career.

Founder-members of the Actors' Company prepare for a show. Ian McKellen is at the back on the right and Edward Petherbridge next to him. This company chose its own plays and hired its own directors, reversing the usual casting process

The touring fringe company '7:84'. It is said that 7% of Britain's people own 84% of the nation's wealth. This company's plays stress that idea

For most actors now, first jobs come on the 'fringe'. Two decades ago New York realized that fringe theatre was the only economical way to stage plays and give actors and directors the chance to work. Big theatres were too costly, and if plays failed a lot of money was lost. Britain then discovered this 'alternative' theatre and today West End managements are quite willing to present shows begun on the fringe. Very few impresarios are reckless enough or rich enough to gamble big money on the success of a stage show: it is far better to let it prove its success before installing it in a fashionable theatre. The people who own the theatre buildings are the ones who finally decide what play goes on. No matter how dedicated the artists are it is the weekly rental that decides the fate and fortune of the play. Tiny theatres have tiny rentals and only need a small staff to run. London's Drury Lane or New York's Palace Theater in Times Square need to take a lot of box-office money to pay their overheads.

Equity

Showbusiness is such a jungle and such a rich ground for swindlers, confidence-men and liars that a trade union is the only possible organization that can begin to protect the performer. Actors want to act and very often they are not able to serve their own best interests: how can they when they have so little power and so much responsibility? Managements, naturally, want to make money and only some are as interested in the quality of the show as they are in whether it is saleable or not. Success is the pursued goal; art comes a long way second. This isn't surprising when audiences are so lazy about watching live plays. Vast advertising has to drum into people's heads that a show is worth seeing, and newspaper critics play a vital part in whether a show succeeds or not.

British and American Equity work incessantly trying to negotiate and untangle the complicated legal (and illegal) clauses of contracts for artists in all forms and concerns of show business: stage plays, television, cinema, commercials, *son et lumière*, living costs, repeat fees, and, at the moment, the complex problem of video-cassette sales and the artist's share of 'pay' television. Equity not only lays down a basis for payment but insists upon certain standards of hygiene and comfort for artists (though backstage at some New York theatres conditions are

Max Stafford-Clark talks to playwright Caryl Churchill. He is now Director of London's Royal Court Theatre which, since the days of Bernard Shaw, has presented new writing

unbelievably bad). Equity is the artist's protector and should be notified when things go awry. All actors pay an annual subscription to belong to Equity and there are many contracts which are not officially Equity-blessed. When you begin to act, especially on stage, you will do many plays that do not carry with them an Equity contract: very likely they will carry nothing except experience—not even lunch!

You do not automatically become an Equity member when you begin work. To belong to it you must first get a role that carries with it an Equity contract. You are then placed on a probationary period and when you have worked as an actor for about forty weeks you can become a full member of the trade union and benefit from its protection. The trouble is that the world is full of *probationary* members because managements will hire cheap beginners; thereafter it is harder to find properly paid work.

What Kind of Work?

When you take the ridiculous plunge and call yourself a professional actor the first thing you have to get used to is *not* working. There's a paradox! At theatre school you will have been run off your feet, totally absorbed by the routine of class, role, singing and dancing instruction, elocution, stage history and all the rest of it. You may have been given some stage-management experience and taught about understudying or wig-making (should your acting work become *too* scant). You will have been stretched by performing and will have absorbed a great deal in three short years. You'll have liked some teachers and not others, and you should have discovered certain things about yourself as a performer and how your future development might shape. Now, in the real world, you will tramp the streets seeking an acting job anywhere, from anyone. And you'll have to live, so you will find temporary work, typing or waitressing or doing night-security or playing a bar-room piano. Luck, persistence and courage are the only qualities that will make you fight it out; added to a belief that should a part come your way you will play it better than Bernhardt or Jason Robards!

But all this still sounds romantic. Let's fill in some details. You have been trained to act and are hoping to get your teeth into works by Shaw, Pirandello, Ibsen, Chekhov or some such master. Instead, an agent or agency might offer you ushering at a furniture exhibition or modelling for a magazine or a T.V. ad. You'll probably do it, because the borderline between acting and this kind of work is thin and you might meet somebody useful, and it *is* vaguely creative—isn't it? Well, only you can answer that question: is huckstering in a department store enough like acting not to make you feel humiliated? Do you think it wiser to spend the week-end at a friend's pool because it is just possible that a vague relation may drop by who is married to—a casting director in Hollywood! You can see that you must have remarkable resilience to survive in this way.

Two great actors in their heyday: Sir Ralph Richardson as Falstaff and Sir Laurence (now Lord) Olivier as Justice Shallow, in Shakespeare's *King Henry IV* at the Old Vic, London, 1945. Make-up can do miracles!

More importantly, you must have a very firm idea of where you are going and what you really want to do.

For a true actor, acting work of any kind is better than not acting. It doesn't matter where it is, however rural or far-removed from New York, Los Angeles or London. You must believe that if you go and do some good work somewhere, you will not only be doing what you really want to do but will be storing up solid experience for better chances when they come along. One thing is certain in show-business: when the opportunity of a good part comes along the person most likely to be able to handle it and make a success of it is the person who has practised his craft. Experience is the gold of show-business. Money you should seek in another job.

Stages

But what is the 'serious' actor or actress doing looking for great roles no matter where they are offered? Why do human beings want to put on a mask (of Hamlet or Hedda Gabler) instead of settling down with a solid job, marriage and children? You can't expect the person who wants to act to have the things in life that other people seek. The actor seeks something else: an identity and the opportunity to be close to ideas and thoughts that have shaped the world and gone some way towards making modern man imagine he is master of his own destiny. By adventuring into great literature and the truths about human nature that the best dramatists have revealed the actor is blessed and privileged in a way that many other people are not. As a result he must, perhaps, forgo the ease, luxury, and some of the comfort that others get from security and wealth. The actor's joy is not in having but in giving. If as an actor you are a success on the stage you will devote your life to audiences. You will have to keep your memory intact to learn lines and your voice in fine condition to please people's ears, and your strength will be preserved by keeping decent hours. To put it practically, you have to serve an author and your colleagues. That is why you must remain in good shape with keen wits. Every professional depends on every other professional, otherwise the show may close, and you are back again hunting for a job.

Stage parts are so hard to come by that they must be given all your love and all your thought. The moment the curtain goes up—*that* is the time to show the world what you can do. Many people forget this and it *is* easy to forget. The actor's daily routine is so busy with seeing agents and hustling for jobs, keeping in touch with friends to see what's going on, and going to see friends when they get a part, that when at last you are on a stage with a decent role, you may not fully realize that *this* is what acting is all about. This, now. Not the parties and the writing letters and having all those photographs taken with your résumé on the back.

On stage the actor is concerned with the truth of his character and with the shape of the production—the rhythm and speed of scenes—and he is also, somewhere in his mind, conscious of the audience that is sitting out there. He should be able to play what has been rehearsed, but slightly to adjust his performance, if necessary, according to the reactions of whoever has been kind enough to pay to watch. The actor has to be heard and he must make his

The Guthrie Theater in Minneapolis is named after an Irishman who worked in Britain, Canada, the U.S. and Israel—Sir Tyrone Guthrie, a stage director of genius

A performance in Britain's National Theatre with Albert Finney in *Tamburlaine the Great.* This 'Olivier' auditorium has been designed with the ancient Greek theatres in mind

actions apparent to the whole audience. After all, if no audience were there he wouldn't do the play at all would he? He can never forget that they are his patrons, his reason for being there.

The actor has to play in a wide variety of theatres, some huge with a proscenium arch of ninety feet, and some so tiny that cast and audience seem to inhabit the same space. In the English town of Richmond, Yorkshire, there is an eighteenth-century 'doll's house' theatre seating about ninety people, with long benches and gated 'side-boxes' making a tight rectangle. Other theatres seat three, five and even seven thousand people. The actor-audience relationship is of great importance to a successful performance. The Olivier auditorium at the National Theatre in London was built according to the Greek amphitheatre design. At a central point about two-thirds upstage the actor has complete eye-command of the whole house. Manchester's Royal Exchange theatre in Lancashire is a towered circle, where the actor moves round inside a sort of chimney and for the audience the physical experience is very exciting. In the past theatres were made bigger and bigger for profit. Today, musical shows need big stages, as do ballet and opera, but intimate plays set on large spaces can suffer immensely. Microphones are used in most theatres now, and so are very sophisticated methods of amplification. But if you see a well-acted play in a space intimate enough *not* to require microphones (and if the actors' voices are good enough) you will enjoy the naturalness, vocal colour and command performers can give to the play in a theatre of 'human' size. Being able to see the detail of a performance is important too, and this is made easier in a smaller theatre.

Voice

Acting is all to do with communication and that is why the actor-audience relationship is so vital however much it is ignored and misunderstood by commercial managements and even some directors. Acoustics, as any orchestral musician will tell you, are *not* a science. They cannot be fully measured when building an auditorium. The quality and resonance of the sound inside a building cannot be known until the hall has been built and tried out; then various adjustments can be made, like 'baffling' or using special material to 'soften' or 'harden' sound. Most theatres have 'dead spots' where sound does not carry, and this is an accident in the design or the materials used. Sometimes small theatres need powerful vocal projection, while, as happens in an outdoor amphitheatre, large spaces can be 'reached' by well-enunciated and articulated voices.

The actor places nearly as great importance on voice as does the singer. The Royal Shakespeare Theatre at Stratford-on-Avon stands beside a river and when the autumn mists rise from its banks many members of the company creep round in scarves hoping not to get the 'dreaded vapours' on to their vocal chords. Professional actors have to understand how their voices work so they can use the voice correctly without harming it, and so they can take the necessary remedy if it lets them down. It is astonishing what the human voice can do, how strong and tough it is. Whether it will serve the actor

A Royal Shakespeare Company touring version of Brecht's *The Caucasian Chalk Circle*. The poor 'baby' is nearly pulled to pieces in the play by two women claiming to be its mother

well—and in the theatre the voice is his most important instrument—depends very largely on how he uses it and whether he 'produces' it correctly, without placing strain on the vocal chords and with enough supportive breath to breathe easily, the lungs used like bellows blowing up a fire.

Action

Performing is a little like being a soldier going into battle. The 'harsh urgency' of theatre places the actor in a highly vulnerable situation. The curtain is up, a thousand people have paid to watch—what is it he is going to do that will at least keep their interest and perhaps 'move' them, make them laugh or cry? Of course the actor may be an exhibitionist but he always has to work for his supper. He has to deliver there and then, there can be no delays, excuses or strikes (well he *can* strike—there has been strike in America over the important question of cable T.V. fees), but for the actor who loves theatre a strike is the last thing he would ever contemplate, however pressing his grievance. Theatre is made by many people all contributing talent and time. The actor not only tries for himself but for everyone else concerned with the show. This is why professionalism—the

Arch-professional Sir Laurence Olivier meets cinema-goddess Marilyn Monroe in the film *The Prince and the Showgirl*

attitudes and concern of the professional—is so valued by those who work in the theatre. They all rely upon each other, both before and after the curtain goes up. Imagine the poor author pacing up and down the town (like W. S. Gilbert on the first night of his Savoy operettas) powerless to influence events further and relying on artists and musicians to make a success of it.

However vain and conceited actors or actresses may be they have no right to hamper other people's livelihoods. Arriving late at a theatre is unforgivable, as is being late 'on set' for a movie. In most actors this kind of behaviour will not be tolerated and 'stars' who indulge in it are very often disliked by those with whom they work. The public, of course, like reading about the latest fracas or scandal about this or that superstar. Many simple people live through their screen or television idols and sometimes the characters in a soap-opera interest them more than their own families or neighbours. But sensible people realize that dramatic characters are fiction and that their place is on stage or screen, portrayed by an actor and actress. One great critic of theatre, Dr. Samuel Johnson, said that any man who imagines himself anywhere else than in a theatre while a play is performed is mad. But we are all given to enjoying the fantasy of plays and films, and we do this by what Samuel Taylor Coleridge, another great critic and poet, called 'the willing suspension of disbelief'.

This problem of believing or not in drama troubled Bertolt Brecht, too. He directed his plays so as constantly to remind audiences that they were *not* to believe in what they saw and heard; rather they should attend in a *critical* way to what was going on, more as if they were listening to a debate than spectating at a 'piece of life'. All this comes back on to the actor who, from one job to the next, must play in different styles and work for very dissimilar minds, absolutely real in one piece and a kind of puppet in

the next. Hamlet says that acting should 'hold a mirror up to Nature', but there are all kinds of mirrors, distorting ones too, and it is possible to look even at your own reflection in different lights and with different mental attitudes. The self-portraits of painters are flattering, self-disgusted, honest or more interested in the play of light than in the subject-matter. Rembrandt kept painting himself at different ages, knowing that human beings do change. The actor, if he can, must remain adaptable and receptive to change, for he will be asked to perform in a variety of styles and to work with very contrasting minds. Writers and directors seek, on stage or film, to paint their picture of the world. The actor is part of someone else's vision.

Keeping physically fit is very much part of the actor's readiness. Who knows when and where you'll go and indeed what you'll be asked to do? A leading

Marlon Brando playing Stanley Kowalski in the film of Tennessee Williams' *A Streetcar Named Desire*, with Vivien Leigh. Brando is a pupil of the Method approach to acting which is based on Stanislavsky's teaching

actor has to call upon great reserves of physical stamina. Making the most of whatever body you have is essential for a performer. In America actors have long realized that only by continual training and acting classes can the irregular life of the professional be given some cohesion. British actors are just waking up to this fact. Hitherto there has been a more solid and accessible structure of live theatre to go into, but now, in London especially, many actors, including established 'stars' have realized that they need daily limbering classes (dancers of course *have* to do daily training), and that they benefit from keeping in touch with other professionals of equal status in all areas of work: text classes, singing, dancing and allied skills like tumbling, mime, or even learning through Yoga and the 'Alexander' method how to relax fully and keep in touch with their own inner selves.

Acting, which for beginners is so often a thing of released energy and *joie de vivre* becomes, the older one gets, an attitude of mind, indeed the controlling of mental processes. You have to continue *wanting* to act. Supposing some personal tragedy has hit you one day: you will be expected to go through with the performance that night. Some people think that the excitement and fear aroused by performing is in itself a remedy for ills, a kind of medicine which produces a change of chemistry to throw off minor ailments. When you are in the run of a play your whole life revolves around the evening performance. The call of the audience may take precedence over other people in your life. The actor tries to give 'his all' to an audience each evening.

A recent play *The Dresser*, by Ronald Harwood, paints an enthralling portrait of one of the last of the Victorian-minded actor-managers. He is nearly mad and all his striving, playing the great parts of Hamlet, Lear and Macbeth, has not brought him contentment. He says he is 'driven' by inner forces to continually scale the mountains of his craft, and yet now old and weak, he feels that each performance becomes a nightmare for him. This is not the world of the amateur, and sadly, even today it is possible to end up lonely or forgotten after a lifetime's service to the theatre.

Opposite: Freddie Jones makes up on stage in *The Dresser*. The old actor has to play *King Lear*, but can he still do it?

Showbusiness divides between those who think of it primarily as a means of getting rich, no matter how, and those whose artistic sense is paramount. Everybody—actors, writers and producers—may have to choose between one or the other. Commercialization is a dangerous force in showbusiness because it usually leads to compromise and away from creative truth. The actor is always left vulnerable to the public's gaze, to be assessed by them in the name not only of entertainment but of art. There are, dotted all round the business, people who keep alive what is good and great. But what a vast and various trade it is that has the gaudy glitter of Radio City's Rockettes at one end and the dedicated courage of Athol Fugard's Market Theatre in South Africa at the other! Perhaps you are now wondering if there is a place for you in the wide showbusiness world, with its studios and offices as well as its stages and film-cameras. It is quite possible to work in showbusiness and not be a performer. You can write, administrate, be a secretary, build scenery or work in a publicity office. There are scores of jobs you might like to do which have nothing to do with performing, or at least everything to do with it except the spotlight, the vanity and the fear.

Some people in showbusiness despise performers, as though without them the whole business would be a lot more trouble-free and pleasant. Performers have to be fussed over and listened to, they have to be found accommodation and paid. While performers are in touch with the public all the other people in showbusiness are 'behind the scenes', and this can be a cause of deep resentment. Actors are called 'children' and they are held guilty of shallow and irresponsible behaviour, but very often this kind of criticism stems from envy. The actors get all the fun and fame, but what about all the people without whom the whole thing would not be possible?

But it is the actor who must go from one medium to another in search of work (no permanent office for him with its friends and its security). It is the actor who travels, lugging his suitcases with him, perhaps even his family! It is the actor who must radiate charm and be ready to act whenever a director clicks his fingers. It is the actor who must

sign autographs and who must try to piece together a career whether he is a film-star or humble beginner. He goes from employer to employer like a mercenary soldier and does his job, he hopes successfully. Then he must move on to where his next job is coming from, and always remain ready not only to act but to do many other things a performer may be asked to do. Finally, it is the actor who must face the response of the world, be it ecstatic adoration or bad fruit and rotten eggs.

The Royal Shakespeare Company's great success *Nicholas Nickleby*, an adaptation of Charles Dickens' novel. Here the Vincent Crummles travelling players pose for a 'Victorian' photograph

Acknowledgments

The illustrations are reproduced by kind permission of the following: Spectrum Colour Library 2; Ronald Sheridan's Photo-Library 3; The Mansell Collection 5, 6, 10, 17, 87; Peter Newark's Historical Pictures 8, 13, 20; Scala/Vision International 11; Royal Shakespeare Theatre, Stratford-upon-Avon (Photo: Gordon Goode) 14; Mary Evans Picture Library 16, 18, 21, 22; Sovfoto/Eastfoto 25, 26; National Theatre (Photo: Nobby Clark) 28; National Film Archive 30, 33; BBC Hulton Picture Library 31, 35, 68, 69; Kobal Collection 32; Aquarius Film & TV Picture Service 36, 107; Crouch Associates 39; BBC Copyright Photograph 42, 56–7; Rex Features 45, 48, 52; NBC Photo 54 (bottom); Reg Wilson 78; Lesbert of Exeter 84, 85; The Questors Theatre, Ealing 89; Martha Swope, New York 90; Shaw Theatre (Photo: Nobby Clark) 92; John Timbers 94; The Drama Studio, Ealing 95; Nigel Luckhurst 97; 7:84 Theatre Company (England)/Photo: Mike Laye 98; Paul Roylance 99; Robert Harding Associates (Photo: John Vickers) 101; The Guthrie Theater, Minneapolis, Minnesota 103; Denys Lasdun & Partners (Photo: Donald Mill) 104; Royal Shakespeare Company (Photo: C. Davies) 106; Ronald Grant 108–9; John Haynes 111; John Napier/Royal Shakespeare Company 113.